LAUNCH IN 5

Taking Your Idea from Lightbulb Moment to Profitable Business in Record Time

WILL RUSSELL

Foreword by Orvel Ray Wilson,
co-author of six books in the legendary
Guerrilla Marketing series, selling more
than 26 million books in 63 languages

NICHOLAS BREALEY
PUBLISHING

BOSTON • LONDON

First published in 2022 by Nicholas Brealey Publishing
An imprint of John Murray Press

An Hachette UK company

26 25 24 23 22   1 2 3 4 5 6 7 8 9 10

All images courtesy of Russell Marketing

A CIP catalogue record for this title is available from the British Library

Library of Congress Control Number: 2022932542

ISBN 978-1-3998-0170-6
US eBook ISBN 978-1-3998-0450-9
UK eBook ISBN 978-1-3998-0171-3

Printed and bound in the United States of America.

John Murray Press policy is to use papers that are natural, renewable, and
recyclable products and made from wood grown in sustainable forests.
The logging and manufacturing processes are expected to conform to the
environmental regulations of the country of origin.

John Murray Press Ltd   Nicholas Brealey Publishing
Carmelite House   Hachette Book Group
50 Victoria Embankment   53 State Street
London EC4Y 0DZ   Boston, MA 02109, USA
Tel: 020 3122 6000   Tel: (617) 263 1834

www.nbuspublishing.com

CONTENTS

FOREWORD

Most Americans—three in five—dream of starting their own business, but most of them will never take the risk. Of those who do, many will fail. But take heart. This book, like the landmark Guerrilla Marketing series, will show you multiple ways to launch and maintain a successful business—reduce your risk, hedge your bets, and attract an early following of loyal customers using simple, low-cost strategies that anyone can apply.

While it's mostly young entrepreneurs we see on the cover of magazines, many of us get the entrepreneurial bug in our 40s, 50s, or even later in life. We finally have the time (and the resources) to start that dream business. But the internet changed everything, and traditional marketing channels have been pushed aside for both young and old. In this book, you'll hear about the latest tools for creating copy, building websites, testing landing pages, and analyzing web traffic. You'll see how to do the math to know exactly what your return on investment from your launch marketing will be. If phrases like "landing pages," "conversion rate optimization," and "lead funnels" freak you out, you'll find the answers here.

"Measurement" is one of the keystones of effective marketing, and this book is all about the data. But don't let that scare you—it's a tool that's easy to master. This book will show you how to discover what your potential customers truly value, and how to speak to them in the terms that matter most to them. You'll learn how to prove that your idea is a good one (or how to adjust it if it's not). It will show you how to develop a following of passionate fans even before you launch. And it will show you how to build an army of loyal customers.

Before you take out a second mortgage and bet it all on a business idea, follow author Will Russell's Five-Step High-Profit Launch System in this book to virtually guarantee a successful launch and make your entrepreneurial dreams come true.

—Orvel Ray Wilson

CHAPTER ONE

Entrepreneurship for the Risk-Averse

T'S ALMOST SIX years to the day that the idea of quitting my 9-to-5 job and starting a business began to take seed in my mind. Just like I was back then, perhaps you're currently spending your days as an employee dreaming of being your own boss. Maybe you've had an idea for a product or a business in the back of your mind for a while and you're finally ready to turn it into something real. Or it might be the case that you've discovered this book as an accomplished entrepreneur with a breadth of experience building products, brands, and businesses.

Whoever you are and whatever your journey so far into the world of entrepreneurship, with every new launch, project, and business idea comes fear: a fear of failure, a fear of rejection, a fear of the unknown, and a fear of losing the life or career you've worked so hard to achieve. The following pages introduce you to launch strategies that will forever change how you pursue new ideas, removing the fear, reducing the risk, and re-engineering what it is (and what it takes) to become a successful business owner. Welcome, and thank you for being a part of it.

I'm a direct person. Small talk is my nemesis. I like to be frank, honest, and get straight to the point. So, allow me to do so right from the get-go. You're probably thinking something along the lines of: "Is this book for me?" "Should I listen to this guy?" "Is my time reading this going to be time well spent?"

My response to all three is a thundering Yes!

Allow me to explain.

You've probably picked this book off a shelf or are perusing it online because you're a relative newcomer to the world of entrepreneurship and have an idea you'd like to make reality. Perhaps you've recently launched (or are about to launch) your own business, have a side project that you dream of turning into a full-time gig, or have been sitting on an idea for a long time and are seeking inspiration and knowledge to help you take the next step.

As I write these first paragraphs, we're approaching two years into a raging pandemic, and, according to the US Census Bureau, applications for new businesses are rising at the fastest rate in more than a decade. Many people, just like you, have finally decided to act on their dreams of being a business owner. They have had their eyes opened over the past couple of years of lockdowns and remote work. They now see what work-life balance can be like when you don't have a manager breathing down your neck, and when you have the independence and flexibility in your schedule to create a happier life for you and your family. While most are following a dream, many others find themselves out of the workforce due to layoffs and are left pursuing self-employment through no fault of their own. Whether it's by choice or necessity, millions of people are now embarking on the route of entrepreneurship for the first time.

What's more, some experienced entrepreneurs are seeing a whole new world for the very first time. Brands that have focused on offline products and given little regard to their online presence for years have finally been forced into the digital world. Networking, conferences, in-person meetings, and events have been put on the back burner (perhaps never to return, at least not at the same level as pre-pandemic). For businesses that relied heavily on these real-world platforms for marketing, sales, awareness, media, and product launches, it's been a rude awakening. Many have been left scrambling to transition successful offline strategies online, with little time to focus on what that means in practice on a day-to-day basis. Big brands move slowly. Like a tanker turning in an ocean, any type of change is a slow, difficult maneuver. However, thousands of successful brands and entrepreneurs now find themselves on a learning curve and in the midst of an experience that feels more like a kayak being tossed around in a storm, and less like the stability of a tanker devouring the waves.

Given this pandemic-driven period of high unemployment, the shift online, and more isolation than we've experienced in generations, the time for a new type of entrepreneurship is now. It's a type of entrepreneurship that doesn't require access to Silicon Valley, venture capital, or years of work before turning a profit. Instead, it's:

- A type of entrepreneurship that's accessible to anyone with an idea, perseverance, and a problem they're passionate to solve.
- A type of entrepreneurship that doesn't require big risks or big investments.
- A type of entrepreneurship for the high school student learning the ropes, the young professional looking to quit the rat race and create their own successful business, the mom or dad seeking to expand their hobby, or those of an older generation excited to finally pursue their dreams.

If any of that piques your interest, then this book is for you.

Risk-Averse Entrepreneurship

A common belief among newcomers to entrepreneurship is that being risk-averse is a liability. Most books about starting a new business are full of quotes that glamorize risk: "You miss 100 percent of the shots you don't take" (attributed to Wayne Gretzky, hockey legend), "The biggest risk is not taking any risk" (allegedly said by Mark Zuckerberg, founder of Facebook), and "To win without risk is to triumph without glory" (Pierre Corneille, 17th-century French dramatist). Popular wisdom has glamorized risk and deemed it necessary for a new idea to become a successful business. It's a romantic image, one that is perceived as inspiring, heroic, and brave.

Yet, as a result, first-time entrepreneurs are often willing to take make-or-break risks, even when they can't afford failure. In this pro-risk culture, many entrepreneurs make huge, often dangerous leaps, because doing so—risking everything—is the norm.

The first thing you need to do is get over what's known as "Imposter Syndrome" (feelings of self-doubt). You might be feeling it right now, in fact, asking yourself whether you're the type of person who's qualified enough to even be a successful entrepreneur. Later in this book, you'll read how I once felt exactly the same way. From one "imposter" to another, I promise you that you *are* good enough. It's down to tenacity, not talent. As Abraham Lincoln once said: "Your own resolution to succeed is more important than any other one thing." Or, in more contemporary language and in the wise words of Dory from *Finding Nemo*: "Just keep swimming."

Early on in my career, I met with a novice entrepreneur who presented me with a prototype of their "world-changing" invention. The meeting was taking place in a Manhattan skyscraper on a sunny August afternoon. I felt excited, like I was no longer an outsider trying to enter the world of startups and entrepreneurship. I felt that a meeting like this must be (and make me) a big deal.

The client and their advisor took me into a luxurious conference room and laid their product out on the meeting room table. My first thought, in all honesty, was: is this it? I was expecting something phenomenal but found myself looking at something incredibly underwhelming. It was like I'd gone to test drive a Ferrari and found a horse and buggy waiting for me upon my arrival. I felt a knot in my stomach, wondering how to tell him that this idea wasn't quite as brilliant as he thought. Before I could say anything, he informed me, tripping over his words in excitement, that he'd gotten a second mortgage on his house to invest in the first production run. The knot in my stomach ballooned and my heart sank. It was obvious, even at such an early stage of learning about the product, that he'd made a serious mistake and a difficult conversation had just become a whole lot worse. As a relative newcomer to the world of entrepreneurship myself, I couldn't fathom why he would take such a risk. Situations like this led me to deepen my investigation into why we glamorize risk and the role it plays in business ownership.

The conclusion I've come to? Most risk is unnecessary for the vast majority of people starting a business. Many in the world of startups and enterprise suggest that risk and entrepreneurship are interconnected, incorruptible, yin and yang. I think they're looking at it all wrong. My argument is this: Risk-aversion, even in the high-roller, fast-paced world of entrepreneurship, ought to be recognized and defined more widely as an asset.

It's not that I believe risk is entirely avoidable. It's not, of course, and life is full of risk. What I do believe is that there is a huge difference between taking risks because that's what you think has to happen for success and being smart about the risks you take on your path to success. Many new entrepreneurs fall into the former category because that's what they see day-after-day in magazines, in news, and on social media. In fact, in the research for this book, hours were spent poring through articles about entrepreneurs and risk. It's no exaggeration to say that 99 percent of what was discovered focuses on—and glorifies—taking big risks. Try it for yourself: search Google for "quotes about entrepreneurship risk" and see what comes up. The only risk-aversion or risk-management quotes that come up are related to investing in the stock market, not entrepreneurship.

The best-selling author and organizational psychologist Adam Grant presents a similar argument in his book *Originals: How Non-Conformists Move the World*, suggesting that as much as successful entrepreneurs seem to crave risk, they actually prefer to avoid it. "To become original, you have to try something new, which means accepting some measure of risk," Grant writes. "But the most successful originals are not the daredevils who leap before they look. They are the ones who reluctantly tiptoe to the edge of a cliff, calculate the rate of descent, triple-check their parachutes, and set up a safety net at the bottom just in case."

He presents an eye-opening example of this with online eyeglass maker Warby Parker. In 2009, the founders approached Grant about becoming an early investor. But, because they weren't working at their startup full time (they were students at the time) and had accepted jobs post-graduation as a backup plan, Grant assumed they weren't committed enough and declined the offer.

With hindsight, Grant reflects: "When I compared the choices of the Warby Parker team to my mental model of the choices of successful entrepreneurs, they didn't match. [...] In my mind they were destined to fail [...] If they truly believed in Warby Parker, they should drop out to focus every waking hour on making it happen." He continues: "But in fact, this is exactly why they succeeded."

They didn't go full steam ahead with only a plan A, but instead they covered their bases, hedged their bets, and minimized the risk of failure. People often say you must "burn the boats" in entrepreneurship (a quote alluding to the practice where an invading force, having landed in a hostile country, destroys their own ships so that their only options are to conquer the country or be killed). This approach implies that having a plan B is a weakness. Screw that. Having a plan B, a plan C, a plan D, and a plan E is a strategy more likely to lead to success. Risk-aversion is a strength, not a weakness.

Indeed, Grant and I are aligned on this fact. He introduces his readers to a 2014 study by Joseph Raffiee and Jie Feng that presents data supporting risk aversion as a personality trait for new entrepreneurs. From 1994 to 2008, the two researchers tracked a group of would-be entrepreneurs to find out whether a new entrepreneur would be better off quitting a stable job with its regular paycheck and going all in or taking a safer path and working a hybrid model (keep a full-time job while pursuing a business idea on the side) for a period of time. Their research indicated that new entrepreneurs who quit their full-time day job and go all-in on their business idea are more likely to fail than those who continue to work for their employer while pursuing their business idea as a side gig (those who keep a plan B). To be more specific, those who kept their day jobs were 33 percent less likely to fail in their new venture. That's an astonishing difference and the opposite of what many believe to be true in the world of startups and entrepreneurship.

This outcome supports the conclusion of the founding team at

Warby Parker, too: "By the time we were ready to launch and I had to make the decision this was something we were ready to do full time, it didn't seem risky. It didn't feel like I was taking a big leap of faith," Warby Parker co-CEO Dave Gilboa says in Grant's book.

How did the choice to be risk-averse turn out for them? Well, Warby Parker went public in 2021 and ended its first day trading with a $6.8 billion valuation. Not too shabby for a group of risk-averse entrepreneurs.

The message is clear: the most successful entrepreneurs take the risk out of risk-taking.

I created the Five-Step High-Profit Launch System to help new entrepreneurs minimize the consequences of failure—minimize their risk—when launching a new business. It's about taking smart risks and safe risks, not unnecessary, foolhardy risks that many in the world of entrepreneurship space seem to worship. After all, not every idea will succeed. As many as nine out of ten businesses will fail.[1] With the COVID-19 pandemic resulting in more companies forming than ever before, we should be expecting more failures than ever before in the coming years. If the stock market is dropping rapidly, Wall Street can halt all trading to avoid catastrophic losses. As an entrepreneur, you can do the same. By halting a doomed business idea quickly, you can protect yourself from incurring your own devastating losses. The sooner you can determine whether or not people will actually pay money for your product or service, the sooner you can move forward along a successful path or shut your idea down and move on to another one—saving yourself blood, sweat, money, and tears, and saving investors thousands or even millions of dollars.

The system you'll read about in this book has been put to use by thousands of entrepreneurs and launch campaigns. It has generated tens of millions of dollars in revenue for first-time entrepreneurs and new product ideas within just a month or two of their launch days. It was used to help brilliant companies like WeatherFlow raise $2.1 million for the launch of their revolutionary personal weather system, and OneClock generate $1.1 million for the launch of their minimalist analog timepiece. It helped entrepreneurs like Cat Adalay, founder of Shine, and Omar Abu-Shaaban, founder of EDASI, sell out of their first production runs before their products even hit the market. It has been refined, renovated, and renewed many, many times over the years, as each launch provides new learnings. With this book, I'm sharing those learnings with you. No need to start from scratch or reinvent the wheel. Instead, use my successes (and failures, too) to build the right foundation for your own future.

Ultimately, the system you will learn in this book will enable you to test a new business idea out in the world, learn if and why people will pay money for it, and, depending on the answers to those questions, launch it in the most effective and profitable way—the risk-averse entrepreneur's guide to taking your idea from lightbulb moment to profitable business in record time.

You might still be thinking that "risk-averse entrepreneur" is an oxymoron, but I'm living proof. While my launch marketing agency isn't on the same level as Warby Parker, my own experience starting a business is a clear example of risk-averse entrepreneurship at work. Before I decided to start my business, it took several months of informational interviews with other business owners to finalize the decision in my mind. Like many readers, the fear of the unknown (and potential loss) was paralyzing: What if it all went wrong? What if I failed miserably? Once the decision had been made to embark on this journey, it still took another six months of preparation, planning, and research before finally giving notice to my employer and making the leap into this new world. In fact, I was even able to secure a three-month freelancing role with my employer to support them during my transition and provide them time to find the right replacement. My full-time employer became my first official freelance client! By committing to a freelance role during the transition, I had protected myself from a situation where I had zero dollars coming in during the early days of entrepreneurship. Like the folks at Warby Parker, I chose to hedge my bets and prepared backup plans, rather than burn any boats.

My strategy has always been to remove risk. And no doubt I've missed out on some opportunities with this trait. If I'd had the nerve to jump on the Bitcoin bandwagon when I first learned about cryptocurrency, I might be retired and living in Costa Rica by now. Yet I would still argue I've come out on top. I learned that my pragmatic nature is one of my most valuable assets. An aversion to risk has helped me to dodge many bullets and always ensured I could walk before I started to run, which has proven key in creating a solid foundation for a successful business and the launch system at the core of this book.

For the vast majority of us, in this day and age, when we think of launching we think of launching an online business. For that reason, the route of launching an online, profitable business is the journey this book focuses on. However, it would be remiss of me not to acknowledge that you can use the system in this book to pursue any money-making or purpose-driven venture, whether it's a product, event, business, app, or anything else.

Certainly, bringing an online business to life is the most common form of launch, but it's not the only one. How about the hobbyist who wants to launch a new art project and requires a small investment to develop the business further or the amateur pastry chef looking to bring in a bit of extra cash with their community bake sales? Anyone can use the system and strategies in this book.

As you begin working through the first few chapters, you will come to a fork in the road with three possible, preliminary outcomes in the early journey of your idea, all of them occurring quickly (in less than one month) and at a low cost (less than a few thousand dollars, at the high end):

1. You'll prove that there is a market for your idea, and that your target customers will actually buy what you're selling. Through the strategies you'll employ to prove the profitability of your idea, you'll collect data and insights that will enable you to ramp up and invest more in your business with confidence. You're ready to launch!

2. You'll prove that there is a market for your idea, but the data and insights you'll gather might indicate that you'll need to

make a few tweaks before launching to give your business the best chance of success. In this case, there are one or two specific avenues you'll need to launch through for optimal success. For example, the data might show that a particular type of business-to-consumer (B2C) advertising will not be profitable for you, while business-to-business (B2B) distribution has high potential. Learning that you need to pivot early will set you up for a more successful business launch and a better early growth trajectory.

3.   You'll be unable to prove that there is a market for your idea. The data you'll find may show that the idea you have, in its current form, is not something people are willing to buy in the numbers necessary to make it a sustainable business. This is a harsh reality to face. However, by knowing this early in your journey, you can save tens if not hundreds of thousands of dollars and hours embarking on a venture that is likely to fail. You'll have that much more time and money to invest in a different, potentially more promising, idea and you will have more experience to use going forward.

At this point, you'll be in a position to do one of two things:

- Put your idea to the side due to a lack of validity in the market.
- Double or triple down due to the positive early data you've seen.

The former is tough to stomach, admittedly. It might take time to sink in. Once it has, you'll be more experienced and more prepared for your next venture, while keeping hold of a lot of time and money you would have spent trying to launch a doomed idea. If the latter, you can then proceed with confidence into a successful launch and long-term venture.

This book does not offer opinions or sentiments. It deals with data. However difficult it can be to realize that your world-changing idea is not going to change anybody's world, better to know that sooner rather than later. As an entrepreneur, you will face hurdles and defeats. They are unavoidable. What you can limit is the damage those defeats inflict on you mentally, physically, financially, and emotionally. In the same way that it's better to discover your bath water is too hot by testing it with your hand rather than your entire body, it's better to learn a business idea is unlikely to succeed before you devote months or years to it.

Over the years, I've had to tell many entrepreneurs not to pursue an idea. Some heed this advice, others forged ahead anyway. Through hundreds of launches, thousands of test campaigns, and tens of millions of dollars generated for clients using this system, the recommendation to scrap an idea has never been wrong. Whenever the data put out by the system told someone, "Do not invest time or money in launching this idea right now," but they chose to ignore the data, their later experience has always proven the recommendation correct. Their launch failed to achieve the success they were aspiring toward. If you follow this system, you will protect yourself from catastrophe. To be "right" may not be what you envisioned (after all, that could mean a "do not launch" recommendation), but it will be the truth.

While this book was written in a way that you can progress through chapter by chapter and implement the ideas as you go, you can à-la-carte the chapters, too. Want to skip to Chapter 6 and learn about strategies to convert prospective customers into brand advocates? Need to start with the sales objections listed in Chapter 5 to give your current marketing a kick-start? Or begin by making use of the projection models we highlight in Chapter 3 to estimate your future revenue potential?

No problem. This book has been written and set out in a way that each chapter, and even every section in each chapter, has its own value, independent of the rest of the book. Slice it and dice it as and how you like. Read it in 30-minute increments, one section at a time, or chomp your way through the whole thing in one go. It's your call.

Whether you're thinking about launching a product or brand for the first time or you're an experienced founder, these pages and this system offer something valuable for you.

CHAPTER TWO

Five Launch Steps for Every Idea

N THIS CHAPTER, you'll learn:

- The key steps of the Five-Step High-Profit Launch System:
  (1) Validation, Research, and Strategy
  (2) Audience Acquisition
  (3) Audience Engagement
  (4) Audience Conversion
  (5) Scale and Optimize
- The differentiator of the Five-Step High-Profit Launch System is the utility and replicability across any marketing channel, any industry, and any product or idea.
- What "launch marketing" is and how it's unique to all other forms of marketing.
- Replicability in a system is the most effective way to establish your idea in a constantly evolving environment.
- The landscape of e-commerce marketing evolves at breakneck speed. It is in this world—the world of entrepreneurs and creators—that just one small slip, one shortcut, or one missing puzzle piece can bring your journey to a premature end.
- Entrepreneurship and being a creator don't have to be risky. "Risk-averse entrepreneur" is a term we should use more widely in the business arena.

This will give you an overview of the system, introduce you to the concepts, tools, and strategies in each step, and start to show you how to put it into practice for your idea.

Five-Step High-Profit Launch System

There is no universal definition of "launch marketing," not in the same way there is for "marketing" or "e-commerce marketing." Here's my concise explanation:

Launch marketing is a methodology that helps entrepreneurs swiftly and affordably prove an idea has the merit and potential to become a profitable business, generate early success for that business, and create a solid foundation for the business to grow.

Here's what launch marketing is not: Launch marketing is not simply a case of using general marketing strategies for a launch.

Launch marketing is a specific type of marketing within the broader marketing spectrum. Just like people differentiate between search engine optimization, public relations, and digital advertising as distinct types of marketing, you can do the same with launch marketing and a brand's day-to-day marketing or regular e-commerce marketing. While the platforms and tactics you'll use when launching are similar to those that existing businesses use in their day-to-day, your underlying strategy will be more nuanced, precise, and unique.

A lot of this is due to timing. While other types of marketing tend to prioritize lots of small improvements over a long period, launch marketing doesn't have the privilege of time. Launch marketing usually consists of a four- to eight-month campaign, split into several phases. Only in the final phase is revenue generated, and that phase often lasts a mere 30 to 60 days. Then, the "launch" is over, and an entrepreneur will slow down, refocus, and start to transition their strategies with a nod to long-term planning, customer service, and one-year, three-year, or five-year plans for business growth in mind. However, when you're launching an idea, product, or business, you can't afford to make 100 incremental improvements and take months to get a marketing message where you need it to be. You don't have that long to get something fine-tuned; you have days (or sometimes only hours).

You also don't have time for mistakes. One simple error, such as publishing the wrong piece of content at the wrong time or answering a prospective customer's question incorrectly, can bring an entire launch—months or years of tireless work—down like a house of cards. It's scary! But you're not alone. With the right knowledge and preparation, you can protect yourself from these mistakes and avoid the nightmare scenario of a failed business launch.

The Five-Step High-Profit Launch System consists of five core steps:

1. VALIDATION, RESEARCH AND STRATEGY
Understanding the market and proving that your idea is something the market will be prepared to pay for

2. AUDIENCE ACQUISITION
Finding your potential customers and bringing them into a community

3. AUDIENCE ENGAGEMENT
Sharing information with your community to ensure that potential customers are excited to buy

4. AUDIENCE CONVERSION
Turning potential customers into real-world customers once the idea is launched

5. SCALE AND OPTIMIZE
Growing your sales from first gear to fifth during a successful launch period

These five steps develop within three key phases all entrepreneurs ought to go through when launching a new business: Validation (step 1), Pre-launch (steps 2 and 3), and Launch (steps 4 and 5).

Phase one, validation, is about proving there is a market for your idea (step 1 of the launch system), often also known as "Product Market

Fit." This can happen very early in the conception of your journey. In fact, to start this phase, all you need is an idea and little else. It's all about gaining a better understanding of your target customers, digging into the wider market or vertical for your product, analyzing competitive or similar products in the space, exploring possible pricing and profitability, and determining whether your idea can successfully transition from being a good idea to a viable business.

The most recognized form of validation or product market fit is the focus group. Focus groups are a research technique used to collect data through group interaction. We often see these in television commercials or movies—a group of diverse people sitting around a table in a bare room discussing what they like or dislike about a particular product on the table in front of them. On the other side of a one-way mirror, a gaggle of corporate researchers listen in and take notes on the attitudes and opinions of these potential customers. While focus groups can indeed provide neat insights about the market fit of a new product, I believe them to be an outdated, expensive, and inefficient form of validation. Brands sticking with in-person focus groups, rather than using online validation methods, remind me of how my parents still like to use physical maps, rather than a GPS, on long car journeys. Sure, it can work, but it's an inefficient way of doing things. More on why these are outdated methods in the next chapter.

Once you've proven there's a market for your idea, you'll enter the second phase, pre-launch, which is about presenting your idea to potential customers before the big launch (steps 2 and 3 of the launch system). In this phase, you'll build a group of prospective customers and supporters around your idea and engage with them in a way that generates excitement to buy and helps you to collect feedback about your business before you start it. The famous quotation "Build it and they will come" is old news. You simply cannot expect a good idea or product to be enough to drive a high volume of early success. Potential customers need to be introduced to the product, brought into a community, and supported with any and all resources they may need to make their decision to buy or not to buy. One of the biggest mistakes new entrepreneurs make is skipping any sort of pre-launch marketing work, thinking their idea has enough merit to be successful without marketing preparation. The end result for these folks is always the same: a tremendously disappointing launch.

A recent example of a successful program to acquire and engage prospective customers comes from the stock-trading app, Robinhood. Leading up to the launch of the app, Robinhood invited people to gain access to its private beta, giving them the chance to be among the first to benefit from what was offered. After opting in, users were placed on the waiting list and shown a "thank you" page displaying their position on the waitlist, along with the chance to move up the list by inviting their friends, family, and networks to the app, too. The more people a user got to join, the sooner they would get access to the app. Through introducing this type of marketing in the pre-launch process, Robinhood was able to both acquire and engage prospective users long before the app was even available.

Finally, the third phase is the launch. This is when it all comes together! In phase three, you'll ensure your prospective customers take the final action you want them to take—buying your product (steps 4 and 5 of the launch system). Primarily, your attention here will be focused on converting the prospective customers in your community into actual customers immediately after your product becomes available for them to purchase. Following this, a large part of your attention can transition to finding *new* prospective customers and customers outside of your original community. This third and final phase is the most publicly visible part of your launch. This is what we see with ravenous regularity in our day-to-day lives: Apple launching the latest iPhone, a musician releasing their new album, or a new condo in your neighborhood coming onto the market.

Remember, the launch system described is universal. This system works with any idea, any marketing channel, and any budget. I've seen entrepreneurs use it online and off, from one-person startups to global corporations, with budgets of $50 to $500,000. You can use it in any industry, for any idea.

One afternoon in 2016, I hit the streets of San Francisco with the founder of a technology-related concept (just a drawing on a piece of paper at that point) and asked strangers for their name, email address, and a small fee (less than $10) for future access. That one afternoon of chatting with members of the public, taking down names, and validating the idea in the market soon became Techtonica, a real-life organization that promotes diversity in the tech industry by providing technical training to underrepresented populations and connecting them with hiring organizations. As of this writing, it is still thriving in the Bay Area.

For online entrepreneurs considering a launch in the near future, your launch marketing will probably focus on a few key marketing strategies:

- Paid advertising (such as Facebook ads, Google ads, and Snap ads)
- Digital communication (like email marketing, SMS [text messaging], and chat bots)
- Conversion rate optimization (a focus on making the experience great for the customer, using tactics such as landing page design and improving the customer checkout process).

Currently, these channels are empowering launch marketers like me. While the platforms may change over time, the concepts you'll learn in this book are timeless and can be applied to any marketing channel.

Whatever your big idea and business aspirations, this system can work for you. It is the smartest, safest way to launch a profitable, successful business.

Permanence in an Ever-Changing World

A theme you will see multiple times in this book is replicability: the quality of processes, strategies, and systems to be precisely copied or reproduced. Why is this so important for the launch system and the idea you're launching?

Replicability is the most effective way for a business (both new and old) to attain a level of permanence in a constantly evolving environment. A process, strategy, or system that is created with an ability to be standardized and replicated transcends the change happening around it.

Consider how the online cloud displays a tremendous amount of replicability compared to the traditional method of saving files locally. If you save a document to Dropbox or Google Drive, that document is replicated across your phone, tablet, work computer, home laptop, or an internet cafe 5,000 miles away from where you originally created it. It doesn't matter if you buy a new laptop or replace your phone, if you change jobs or move across the world, or if you want to see that document one day or 20 years from now. Whatever external factors change, the cloud offers replicability and permanence.

Another example of replicability found in the *Harvard Business Review* is the global agribusiness Olam.[1] The company started as a cashew trader, purchasing nuts directly from farmers in Nigeria and selling them to customers in Europe, cutting out the middleman. The systems developed and standardized by Olam in creating this approach (relatively new at the time for this industry) were then replicated in other countries, industries, and products. They built a system that could easily be replicated. As of Q4 2021, Olam has 81,650 employees and a market cap of $4.1 billion.

Whether you're a one-person team or a global corporation, the long-term health and success of your business can be determined by the replicability of your processes.

The Five-Step High-Profit Launch System is built on precisely this concept, with the goal that it can be replicated for any launch scenario. You can apply it to an idea from 50 years ago or an idea 100 years from now, to an idea that costs nothing or to a product priced at six figures, to a team of one starting their first entrepreneurship journey or a multinational corporation's new-product innovation department.

Replicability is closely aligned with another critical concept in my system, too: productization. If you're considering launching a new product, productization is something that should be at the front of your mind. Productization means developing a product, idea, or service into a standardized and cohesive offering, making it more affordable for the creator to deliver it to the customer. It means being able to place that product, idea, or service into the hands or minds of as many people as possible, as quickly as possible, and as profitably as possible.

Perhaps the best-known example of productization is Henry Ford and his game-changing work innovating vehicle production with the moving assembly line. Before Ford, teams of craftsmen and engineers built vehicles by hand. We can think of this method as a service model. This was time-consuming, expensive, and limited the production capabilities of a factory. Ford changed this. Rather than the worker moving to and around the vehicle, Ford's moving assembly line allowed for the vehicle to be taken to the workers. Moving the work to the worker, rather than the other way around, was a better use of time and resources, reducing the time it took to build a car from more than 12 hours to just 90 minutes.[2] In essence, Ford had productized the service model.

Another example that might be closer to home for you is the productization during COVID-19 of traditionally in-person services. Take personal trainers. Before the pandemic, most personal trainers worked with their clients in person. There are only so many hours in a day, which means that a trainer can only take on so many clients if they are booking individual in-person sessions. Now, consider how the shift from in-person meetings to online video meetings enabled personal trainers to productize their offering. Rather than preparing and planning a customized workout plan for one person at an in-person session, trainers could curate workout sessions that they delivered online. Dozens of people could participate in these sessions, resulting in the trainer reaching more people and acquiring more customers much faster and more efficiently than before.

Consider the Five-Step High-Profit Launch System like a recipe. It should exist so that people, just like you, are able to gather the ingredients, work their way through the preparation steps, and end up with a delightful dinner dish. Being able to do it yourself doesn't dismiss the value of experts and the service they provide, as some marketing agencies in the launch marketing space might suggest. After all, Gordon Ramsey would certainly deliver a better culinary experience than I, regardless of the excellence of the recipe. However, a lack of access to a world-class chef shouldn't prohibit anyone from enjoying a quality meal, just like a lack of access to capital or vast expertise shouldn't prohibit people from pursuing their dream and launching an idea into the world. By standardizing the process and making each step replicable, ensures it can be a tool that anyone can use, rather than a service only experts can deliver.

A key question for me in creating this system was always: "If 'X' ('X' being a key tactic used in implementing the system, such as Facebook advertising) disappeared tomorrow, would this system still work?" For the system to have longevity and offer the most value to the most people, the answer has to be yes.

My launch experience over the last few years tends to focus on social media ads and crowdfunding campaigns, as those have been the most fruitful marketing channels in recent times. In this instance, "X" could be Facebook advertising or Indiegogo. If we lose things like these that are currently essential to the system, is the system built in a manner that the item can easily be replaced without adverse effect? Over time, this was put to the test as the Five-Step High-Profit Launch System started to face a number of firsts.

The first time this was put to the test, it happened with step 2 (Audience Acquisition). The entrepreneur had to forego online social media advertising, so we applied the theory of step 2 to a different channel entirely—offline surveying and local events. Through running surveys and asking questions to communities about the particular launch idea, and with groups that represented the client's target audience, we were able to acquire an audience of thousands. No online advertising at all, yet the goal of audience acquisition was successfully achieved.

The first time the system was asked to sell intangible knowledge (such as tickets to lectures or networking events) rather than a physical product, we applied the theories of step 1 (Validation) to better understand how we ought to present the offer to increase the value perception of something that was impalpable. We were able to identify precisely what it was about the intangible knowledge that people most valued and use that to launch a series of standing-only, real-world events across the US.

The first time the system was asked to sell a high price-point product instead of the lower cost home goods on which it was first built, we could easily adapt the system to place more of a focus on step 3 (Audience Engagement). People buying an expensive product need a higher level of engagement from the brand in order to make their purchasing decision. Each phase and step of the system remained the same— it transcends product type or cost. Instead, we nipped, tucked, and stretched a few pieces here and there, and successfully used the system on the launch of a high-cost electric bike.

And, the first time it was asked to deliver a successful launch for a global corporation rather than a new startup, we simply adjusted to allow for slower decision-making, bigger budgets, and the added layers of bureaucracy. It worked. This company sold out of their product within 48 hours.

Like the enduring support fans have for their sports team, despite changes of players, executives, owners, and even home cities, the success of this system transcends and endures. Being flexible and nimble are important, certainly. However, a system that is constantly being reinvented due to external factors cannot offer scalability or permanence. Imagine if Tesla had to create new models depending on the season? Or governments had to rewrite entire constitutions every decade? Possible? I guess. Efficacious? Certainly not.

The Evolution of E-Commerce

When it comes to evolution and change, there are few places we see it more than the internet and marketing. In December 1995, just 0.4

percent[3] of the world's population had access to the world wide web. Ten years later it surpassed a billion users, representing approximately 16 percent of the world. As of autumn 2021, almost 60 percent of the world (4.5 billion) is connected. From one website in 1991 to 1.7 billion today, containing 5.56 billion indexed web pages (and this doesn't include the dark web, estimated to be 400 to 500 times larger than the common internet), the changes we've seen in a relatively short period of time are almost incomprehensible.

Marketing of products and businesses has been a big part of this evolution, with few industries benefiting so much from the data footprint people leave behind online. Just a generation ago, marketing budgets would have focused on three key pillars: television, radio, and print. These channels have become victims of technological advances, with internet giants now dominating marketing budgets. Google advertising revenues accounted for $134.8 billion in 2019, while Facebook ad revenues hit $69.66 billion that same year.[4]

The convergence of the internet growth and marketing evolution becomes most apparent when looking at e-commerce. Take Amazon, as a prime example. It is said to have well and truly killed the high street, or Main Street for those in the US. Nine out of 10 customers now check the prices of a product on Amazon, with more than 12 million products on the site to peruse at the time of writing. What once was an online bookstore is now a must-have marketing channel for almost any merchant.

Another e-commerce platform, Shopify, shows the shift from offline to online by businesses. Starting by selling just snowboards in 2004, it now hosts well over 300,000 online shops for merchants selling all sorts of products and services. And the growth has only gotten faster. Total revenue for Shopify in the third quarter of 2020, peak pandemic, increased 96 percent from the previous year.[5]

It's not just brands tapping into the online sales opportunities provided by rapid technological advances over the last decade, it's individuals, too. In fact, in many cases, brands have stopped creating entirely and instead have become marketers. Brands like Etsy, Upwork,

Fiverr, and Zibbet rely entirely on individuals to create the products or services sold on their platforms, with the role of the brand simply to ensure a consistent stream of customers for those individual creators. Now, anyone with an idea and internet access has the same opportunities to generate income online as the big brands.

Marketing *within* e-commerce has also changed dramatically. It wasn't too long ago that YouTube was free of ads, Facebook was simply a place to communicate and share photos with close friends, and the only way to get online was to sit down at a computer. Furthermore, digital advertising costs have been increasing 100 percent or more, year over year, as measured by CPM (Cost Per Mille/Cost Per Thousand Impressions), while brands have had to shift entire strategies to mobile since the smartphone explosion. How brands reach consumers is changing faster than many people can keep up with.

Let's consider some examples closer to home. In my launch strategies with clients, we run bivariate analyses to determine any relationships between the metrics we see in preparing a client for launch and the sales metrics we see once a launch has occurred. For example, does the cost to acquire a prospective customer before launch have an empirical relationship with the cost to acquire a customer post-launch? Does the rate at which web page visitors sign up pre-launch have a strong or weak correlation with the number of customers acquired post-launch?

Even in my launches with clients over just the past few years, I've seen significant shifts in the relationship between pre-launch (before an idea becomes reality) and post-launch (once the idea is a real-life thing for sale) metrics. One specific example is how the open rate of an email can predict what percentage of your prospective customers will convert into customers.

In 2018, we saw a strong correlation between the open rate of our first email to new prospective customers and the conversion rate of these prospects into actual customers. An analysis of our data shows a correlation coefficient of 0.82. (For those new to this type of analysis: a correlation coefficient of 1 indicates a strong positive relationship, -1 indicates a strong negative relationship, and a result of zero indicates no relationship at all. For the purpose of our analyses, strong relationships, either positive or negative, are very useful in helping us make future projections for a launch campaign.)

Just 12 months later, when reviewing 2019 data, we found that this correlation coefficient had reduced by almost half to 0.42 and, a year later, it had dropped even further still. What this means is that, in 2018, having a strong open rate of our first email to new prospective customers was a positive indicator of launch success. Yet, by 2019, this was no longer the case. In only a few months, the landscape of e-commerce marketing had changed enough that what had been a reliable litmus test for us had to be discarded and replaced.

Fortunately, you will recall that our launch system was built on its capacity to be replicable and malleable, so this particular metric was only one of many numbers we analyzed. It could quickly be replaced by another, with little love lost. It's a sharp reminder, though, of just how fast e-commerce and marketing can change and how processes, systems, and workflows need to be lucid, yet sufficiently sturdy enough to transcend particular strategies or platforms.

Perhaps the biggest inflection point in the history of e-commerce will be the COVID-19 pandemic. Outbreaks around the world shut down shops and locked down citizens, pushing both brands and consumers online to unprecedented levels. Consumers spent $791.70 billion online with US merchants in 2020, up an incredible 32.4 percent year over year, according to US Department of Commerce figures—more than double the 15.1 percent jump the year before.[6]

I would also argue that the supply chain issues caused by COVID-19 have led to an increase in preordering. When a product is offered on preorder, brands can acquire customers and revenue weeks or months before delivering the product to those customers. It's a great way for entrepreneurs to present a product to the market and acquire the funds to produce that product—without taking on the risk of upfront manufacturing costs. This isn't a new idea; it was made popular by crowdfunding platforms like Kickstarter and Indiegogo and has been a core component of launch marketing for the past decade. What

I've seen since the COVID-19 pandemic began, however, are more and more brands turning to preorder as a mainstay of their business model, putting out products on preorder *before* those products are manufactured, rather than the traditional route of selling products *after* they've been produced and when they're ready to ship to customers. What was previously a strategy used mostly by individual creators with limited financial resources has become a go-to for bigger brands looking to reduce their financial risk and protect themselves from the swings of supply chains and shipping costs. You can only imagine this trend will continue, given the acceptance of consumers to this model and the attractiveness of it to businesses.

To return to the comments at the start of this book, the Five-Step High-Profit Launch System is about minimizing risk. If something is at risk of being critically affected by the environment around it, it's, well, it's risky, isn't it? I don't like risk, so any systems I create and work with do their best to remove as much of that precariousness as possible. It all starts with a little research.

CHAPTER THREE

Validate to Create

N THIS CHAPTER, you'll learn how to:

- Research your target audience(s)
- Use how they think, speak, and dream to effectively market your offer to them
- Identify and answer two or three core questions to validate your idea and prove it has potential for success
- Identify Red Flag Metrics (and decide if you need to pivot, adjust, or abandon ship)
- Understand profit margins and various scenarios around profitability

You should do this *before* investing large sums of money in developing and promoting your product or idea. It is recommended you allow yourself about one month to complete the strategies in this chapter.

The Importance of Validation

Arsene Wenger, the longest-serving and most successful manager ever of Arsenal Football Club (and one of my personal heroes), had a bitter rivalry with Sir Alex Ferguson, then-manager of Manchester United

Football Club. At the time, Arsenal Football Club and Manchester United Football Club were the two best teams in the English Premier League.

One afternoon, after a particularly combative match between the two teams, Sir Alex jibed that his team was far better than Wenger's, who, he said, was not deserving of its success. In response, Wenger quipped: "Everyone thinks they have the prettiest wife at home." Sir Alex took it as a personal insult, as you might imagine. It's a rather inappropriate comment, on both a personal and cultural level.

In the context of entrepreneurship, it's a particularly apt quote. Starting out, most new entrepreneurs think that their idea has the potential to be the next big thing. They believe it's a genius solution that can improve the lives of millions of people. This is understandable. If you've created something and are preparing to give it your all, you should be its biggest cheerleader. You should believe it can be a huge success. Otherwise, what's the point?

That being said, there are two red flags I'll often see when a new entrepreneur is advocating for their idea:

1. They believe their idea is for everyone. "Absolutely anyone would find this game-changing, we should market to everyone!"
2. They describe their target audience as a percentage of the total market. "If we can capture just five percent of the market, we'll make a billion dollars in year one!"

These are major pitfalls to watch out for when proving there is a market for your idea. Realistically, no product is for everyone, and setting yourself up with an expectation that you have a target customer base of "the world" is going to end in disappointment. Additionally, potential audience size has nothing to do with whether people will buy your product when you launch. Sure, volume is great—launching a product with 100 million potential customers as opposed to just 1,000 certainly helps—but it is not what makes or breaks a launch. The secret is knowing how to find the groups within your target audience that are most likely to buy whatever you're selling.

When I first met Bob Smith, who wanted to launch his online home goods business, he had fallen into the precise pitfall of having these two beliefs. In his eyes, his idea was sure to succeed, so he'd set everything up for a massive rollout. He'd invested tens of thousands of dollars in kicking off manufacturing, building a team, and creating snazzy marketing videos for his website. Smith had invested zero time and money, however, in determining if this particular product at this particular price point was something that his target audience would actually be interested in.

As it turned out, they were not.

This was an inflection point for my business. I hated seeing Smith fail and wanted to do everything I could to prevent other entrepreneurs from going through something similar. This is when I added the validation component to the Five-Step High-Profit Launch System. By adding this piece to the system, I could help people like Smith find out if their idea was likely to succeed or not, with just a few weeks and a small investment (and, most critically, before embarking on an expensive launch strategy). Since then, the validation process has prevented many entrepreneurs from spending untold thousands of dollars trying to launch ideas that simply won't be successful in the market at that moment in time.

Essentially, validation is a "go/no go" test for your idea. During this period, you'll learn if your business idea can be successful and is worth pursuing, or if it looks likely to fail and you should scrap it. Unfortunately, most ideas are not game-changers. Most founders do not change the world or get featured on the cover of *Time* magazine. Depending on the statistics and industries you look at, between 50 percent to 90 percent of startups fail in the first five years.[1] In the crowdfunding space— an industry devoted to launching new ideas—around 70 percent of launches fail to meet their funding goal.[2]

Failure for a novice entrepreneur is a truly painful experience. I've

seen founders take on loans they can't afford in order to pursue their
dream, only to see the product flop at launch.

As an entrepreneur, the truth is that each new idea is more likely
to fail than it is to succeed. In my capacity as a launch marketer, there
is a responsibility not only for helping entrepreneurs launch successfully, but also for warning them if their idea has clear, obvious, and
insurmountable obstacles to success. Such a conclusion is brutal to
hear for any entrepreneur, so we have to make darn sure such warnings
are right. Each time the Five-Step High-Profit Launch System delivers
a "no-go" recommendation to an entrepreneur, it destroys one of their
dreams. Clearly, there's pain in that. It's horrible to hear. Surely, though,
it's better than letting them destroy their finances and well-being pursuing a doomed idea. Additionally, this means that when a business
idea is a "go," everyone involved can go full throttle ahead, brimming
with confidence.

Go/no-go is a pivotal decision in the journey of an idea. Given the
weight and significance of this decision, you might think it requires
long deliberations, big investments, and all manner of experts. This is
not true. It's possible to complete the actual go/no-go test in just a week
or so, for less than the cost of the latest iPhone (in some cases a *lot* less).

Target Audiences: Who Wants It?

Any validation is going to begin with research. In order to accurately
test the interest level behind your product or idea, you need to make
sure you're testing the right things with the right people. You need to
know who they are and where to find them.

Let's first define who you believe your target audience to be. While
your product idea might serve a wide range of people and audiences,
you must get specific. Much of launch marketing is about prioritization,
and this is a perfect example. Targeting a particular audience doesn't
mean excluding folks who don't fit these precise criteria. Instead,
it allows you to focus your marketing dollars on the prospective

customers most likely to buy from you. Spend some time writing out and describing your ideal customer, using that as a foundation for your target audience research. Specifically, consider:

- Demographics, such as age, gender, income level, family/relationship status, and geography
- Personality, such as their character traits, hobbies, and political stances
- Aspirations, such as career goals or personal dreams
- Challenges, such as day-to-day problems and big, broad fears

To research your target audiences and prove (or disprove) whether you were right in who you believed your audience to be, you must look to actual buyers—those who will be giving you their hard-earned money. One entrepreneur I spoke with claimed over and over again they had validated their health-related product idea by getting commitments from doctors to share this product with their patients. When they launched, they received only a handful of sales (almost entirely from family members). It was a hard and fast lesson for them that product validation must come from those who are making the buying decisions—in this case the patients, not the doctors. Family, friends, colleagues, or even relevant people in your particular market are not your guiding star in whether an idea will sell or not. The potential buyers are.

To kick off your audience research, think about who you believe your target audience to be, then use digital tools such as Google Analytics, Facebook Ad Audience Insights, and online census data to see where your assumptions are and are not correct. When using these tools, ask questions such as: "Do the age, demographics, affluence, and personal interests in the data match who I think the target really is?"

Using the above method, identify four target audiences that you believe will be the best buyers of your product. It helps if these groups are diverse, as this will allow you to collect a wider range of information from your potential audiences. To collect the best information on *who* it really is that wants to buy what you're selling, you also want your audiences to be as isolated from each other as possible. Isolating audiences means setting your marketing up in a way that allows you to discern precisely which audience is causing which result. Consider each audience as its own mini-campaign, in the sense that you must be able to understand the results from each audience independently. One way to do this is to test each audience consecutively, rather than all of them at the same time. You can then easily point to how audience A performed (tested on days 1 and 2) versus Audience B (tested on days 3 and 4). It's not much use getting a great result in validation if you don't know which of your audiences gave you the best result and which performed poorly.

As an example, let's run some mock audience analysis for the validation of a new cleaning technology for home use. Four target audiences we might identify would be:

- Young professionals interested in technology
- Parents with young children, who prioritize cleanliness
- Older adults looking for easier ways to keep their home clean
- First-time home buyers

There will probably be crossover in these audiences (A "young professional interested in technology" may also be a "first-time home buyer"). We want to minimize this crossover as much as possible, though. To do this, we would target a specific group within each audience that we're sure does not exist in another of our audiences. In our example, we would want to exclude technology professionals from our first-time home buyer audience to minimize any crossover between the two audiences so as to keep their results separate.

As you research who your audience is, you will naturally uncover where you can find them. For our cleaning technology example, if Facebook advertising research tools were the most helpful in identifying audiences, that would be a good platform through which to reach this audience. If a real estate company was of great help in understanding a first-time home buyer audience by sharing access to some demographic data from their database, that might be a good route to reach such target audience members.

At the conclusion of your audience analysis, you'll know the four audiences you are going to target in your validation tests and how you will reach them.

Rhetorical Mirroring: What Do They Like About It and How Do They Talk About It?

As you did with your target audiences, you'll also need to identify and validate your key messaging angles (how you will communicate with your audiences). In marketing, we often refer to these as Unique Selling Propositions (USPs). These are the reasons that your product is different from—and better than—your competition. In the validation step, your goal is to determine if your target audiences relate to your USPs enough to merit your starting a business.

There are often a few USPs to consider. After all, the reason one person wants a product may be different from the reason another person wants it. Ultimately, your idea is a solution to a problem your future customers have. Your USPs are what makes your solution better than any other solution in the market. Identify three or four things your product offers that no other product can match, and test these across the audiences you identified earlier in this chapter. In our cleaning technology example, three USPs to test for could be

- The specific technology used in the product (e.g., innovative plasma technology to clean stains) that solves the problem of tough carpet or furniture stains
- The lightweight nature and portability of the product (e.g., portability allows you to take it with you anywhere) that solves the problem of not having access to such a powerful tool when on vacation, traveling for work, or staying away from home

- The ecofriendly and safe elements (e.g., no added chemicals, so it's safe for you, your family, and the environment) that solves the problem of health risks.

With your USPs in mind, it's time to get into the nitty gritty of your messaging. This is where behavioral mirroring, or social imitation, comes into play. We most commonly associate behavioral mirroring with forms of nonverbal communication, like postures, gestures, or facial expressions, such as a young child mimicking the way their parent stands, but we also mirror back words and spoken language. Research supports this method as an effective persuasion strategy,[3] and for good reason—by repeating back what people say, we show empathy and understanding.

Mirroring is a fantastic tool to keep in mind when you draft a marketing message (such as an email, an Instagram ad, a brochure, or a website). It's a way to build trust with your audience and persuade them. A 2007 study on mimicry and persuasion[4] concluded: "Even though consumers might try to resist a salesperson's pitch, being mimicked by that salesperson makes that pitch more impactful." The challenge lies in knowing what messages or rhetoric to mirror in the first place.

First, find where your audience talks about your product or service. For some of us, finding our target audience talking about our product or service is simple: reviews. In the age of the internet, you can find reviews and commentary for any and every type of product or idea. Amazon, Yelp, TripAdvisor, Angi, Thumbtack, Facebook, Twitter, eBay, and Etsy, to name just a few websites that host a plethora of reviews. Reviewers or commenters on those sites may not always be talking about your specific product, but there will certainly be feedback on products very similar (such as your competitors'). When working on the launch of The Quisby, a boutique hostel in New Orleans, and helping them to generate more than half a million dollars in bookings, we found thousands of reviews on TripAdvisor, Booking.com, and Google, talking about similar hostels in the area, so we focused our research there.

If you're selling a service or if your idea isn't a physical product, you may have to dig a little deeper. You may not be able to find reviews of offers similar to yours, so think creatively about where people might be talking about ideas like yours. If your idea is a service, look for books that teach about the service you offer, and what people in your target audiences are saying about those books. People looking for books on a subject in the same category as your idea are likely dealing with the problem your idea solves. Another great place to look is on online forums such as Quora or Reddit.

Once you find where your audiences are speaking about products or services similar to yours, zero in on what it is they're saying. Focus on what problem led the customer to buy the item in the first place and whether the purchase solved that problem. When you understand the problems your target audience is trying to solve with products and services like yours, you can identify the specific benefits and features you should highlight in your own marketing.

Second, collect and categorize the conversation. Look for common trends. You only need to pay attention to the sentences that specifically speak to something good or bad about the product and the problem it is supposed to solve. For example, you don't need to know that Jenny from Maine bought something as a gift for her cousin, just what she thought of the product. Look for problems that many people experience, too. It's not so important if one person has one specific problem they tried to solve using a product like yours, but if 20 people have the same problem, that's valuable information.

As you find these trends, pull comments from your target audience members, and place them in a document, organized by category. For The Quisby, our research into hostels and hotels in New Orleans brought up recurring phrases like "great price," "well worth the money," and "cheaper than anything else I've found." We grouped all of these into a core category: "Affordable."

Here's a look at some of the categories we collected when performing this research in the validation step for The Quisby. In this example, we were looking at positive reviews, but the same process works with

Most frequently referenced positive comments in online reviews

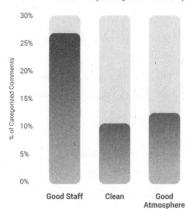

*Parking, pool, Multiple bedrooms, beds

negative phrases. In that case, categorize them by key pain points, not things they liked.

All you need to do to create a graph like this is read through about 50 customer reviews and copy-paste key phrases for those reviews into a document. Then, reread the phrases and identify commonalities. For example, "staff were great," "staff went above and beyond to make our stay special," or "Bob from the front desk was a wonderful guide" all belong in the category "Good Staff." The bar chart clearly notes that the categories of "Good Staff" and "Affordable" stand head and shoulders above the rest.

Once you've categorized all the key phrases into perhaps five to 10 categories, you can see which categories get more or less attention. This tells you which product features will be most important to your customers. In this particular example for The Quisby, 26 percent of positive phrases from customer reviews mention the staff, while only 9 percent refer to meals being provided. We can deduce that a good experience with staff is therefore much more important to the customer than whether or not meals are provided. We can also see how good (or not) competitors are at each.

Third, integrate the categories at a high level. Once you've categorized the comments and identified the trends in what your audiences are saying about your product idea, select the two or three categories that your target audiences are talking about most. Use these as key features and benefits when promoting your idea in your marketing materials. This includes the validation tests you will be crafting later in this chapter.

In the case of The Quisby, the strongest positive trends among our target audiences were the staff and affordability. We made sure to make these features the main messages in our marketing, and integrated them into The Quisby website, social media content, emails, advertising, and all other key marketing channels.

Lastly, use the words and phrases your audiences use in your marketing materials. You can deepen your connection with your audiences by reusing some of the words and phrases you've collected. Essentially, you put these words and phrases from testimonials to the side, and then sprinkle them into your content. For example, when helping to launch Sheets & Giggles, a sustainable bed sheet brand (raising $300,000 in the first few weeks), we found a lot of comments on comparable products using the phrases "so soft," "no pilling," and "breathable." So we integrated this language throughout our marketing copy, with ad headlines such as "Super Soft, Breathable Bed Sheets."

This method can be used for any type of promotion. In Arnold Schwarzenegger's book *Total Recall: My Unbelievably True Life Story,* he shares how he would use the comments and feedback from test screening audiences in his media interview when promoting his movie. He mirrored the language from test screening audiences back out into the broader public, knowing how well it would resonate with his target market.

Knowing how your target audiences speak about the solution you offer, and how they communicate with brands and businesses, is a game-changer. Are they formal? Funny? Do they write long reviews with complicated language or short reviews with slang? Positioning of your offer (how you present your offer, e.g., the language, the images, the price) is everything. Get that wrong and you and your audiences will never connect, as perfect a match as you may be.

Creating Your Brand Tone

Having gotten a clearer understanding of who you want to talk to and how they talk about the problem your idea solves, you'll then need to determine how you want your brand to sound to them. We call this brand tone.

Brand tone dictates how your brand communicates with your audience and therefore influences how you are perceived by others. Your brand tone represents your personality, values, and underlying mission. It's common for new entrepreneurs to skip over this piece of their planning, with many dismissing it as a secondary priority. Consider, though, that your brand tone will influence everything you do. From packaging to copywriting to creative assets, social media to email marketing to print ads, it's the foundation of your presence across any and every platform.

While this may sound complicated, it doesn't have to be. The great thing about defining brand tone as an early entrepreneur is that the brand can simply reflect *you*. The tone and personality you proceed with can simply be the same as your own personality, as is often the case for many entrepreneurs and creators at the start of their journey.

At my launch marketing agency, when we start working with a new client, we'll ask them questions that will provide us with the information we need to accurately represent their brand and create marketing collateral that they feel compliments their own values. These questions are often the first time they've really thought about this side of their business. Their answers won't necessarily deliver a comprehensive brand identity, but they will provide a solid enough foundation on which to move forward.

Below are some examples of such questions. Pause and reflect on them for your brand, even if you feel your brand tone has already been decided.

- What is your elevator pitch? (The elevator is moving; you have 30 seconds to grab attention and take it to the next level. Keep it concrete. Go.)
- What feelings or emotions do you want to invoke in your customers? (What is the emotional brand experience you're trying to deliver?)
- If your brand was a person, how would you describe its personality to someone? (For example, quirky, funny, and edgy? Or genuine, empathetic, formal?)
- What does your competition sound like and how do you want to differentiate? (Sameness is the death of originality. How do you want to stand out from the crowd?)
- Who do you NOT want to be/what do you want to avoid? (Are there phrases we should avoid? Does slang annoy you? Are you anti-emoji?)

In each of the word pairs below, highlight or underline the descriptive word that best fits your brand tone:

1. Funny (increases the power of memory recall and allows you to stand out from competitors) versus Serious (helps build credibility and foster trust but can often lack personality)
2. Formal (makes you appear more authoritative) versus Casual (gives a feeling of personality and friendliness that the formal tone lacks)
3. Respectful (gives a feeling of friendliness and cordiality) versus Irreverent (helps your brand appear confident and authoritative, and even gives a feeling of supremacy over competitors)

4. Enthusiastic (gives a sense of friendliness and helpfulness) versus Matter of fact (gives a feeling of honesty and simplicity, but it can appear indifferent and lacking personality)

Answering a few questions in a simple exercise like this provides tremendous insight into what type of tone needs to shine through. Once you have these simple guidelines for your own brand tone, you can add it to your knowledge of your customers language and start creating the wonderful combination of content that speaks *to* your customers on their level while also representing *your* brand in the way you aspire to be known.

The Copywriting Formula Every Entrepreneur Should Know

Now that you've researched businesses like yours and what people think of them, it's time to run some tests and see what people think of *your* business. If you've never written marketing copy before, now is your time to learn.

Quick Sprout, a popular marketing blog, defines copywriting as: "[T]he art and science of writing copy (words used on web pages, in ads, promotional materials, etc.) that sells your product or service and convinces prospective customers to take action."

Important, right?

Yet many entrepreneurs have experienced copy blockages: sitting in front of a computer trying to write an ad, an email, or web page text for a good hour or more, completely dissatisfied with what's on the page in front of them. It's like being lost for words when you meet someone you admire or having your mind go blank on a first date. You simply can't make the brain connections to get words out!

And when you do finally write something out, it might not even make sense. It doesn't flow. It's not clear.

Truth be told, mind-blanking in marketing is much more of a

problem when you're starting out. Those who have been marketing for a while are not only more effective in writing copy but exponentially more efficient, too.

It's not experience, per se, that makes their writing faster, more cohesive, and far less painful. It's down to one simple fact...

They don't write from scratch. They use templates or formulas to structure their writing.

Copywriting formulae make writing easier and more efficient. A copywriting formula is a framework that structures your writing, so your message has the most impact.

You should be using copywriting formulae whenever you write anything, whether it's your first web page or your millionth advertisement. They eliminate the guesswork that makes bad copy bad (words that don't persuade the reader) and help you write faster and with a much greater chance of success.

There are a million and one copywriting formulae out there for you to use, and I encourage you to explore them all. In this chapter, though, we'll look at just one. A favorite of launch marketers. One I've used (and seen used) time and time again in the launch marketing space.

The Five Rule Recipe

HIGHLIGHT THE PAIN POINT	HIGHLIGHT THE DREAM	MAKE A PROMISE	SHOW PROOF	ASK FOR ACTION

For this formula, start by highlighting the pain point. Paint a picture of the negative scenario the reader is in and the problem that your product, service, or idea can help with. Once you've directed their mind toward this problem, flip it around and paint a beautiful picture of the future. Describe to them the positive scenario when this problem is solved. How will their lives or the world be a better place? Get specific. Then, promise them that you are the person or organization that can make this dream a reality. This is what your offer was made for—to make this transition from pain point to dream real. They don't just need to take your word for it, though. Part four, social proof, is where you show them proof that your claims are fact, not fiction. Finally, don't beat around the bush. Ask them what you want from them. Be explicit with the action they need to take (in launches such as ours, this is often the purchase of a product).

As you plan out your validation, structure your marketing with this copywriting formula. For example, use the Five Rule Recipe to structure a sales web page or a flyer.

A Picture Tells a Thousand Words—A Video Even More

In the modern world, visual content is more engaging and can grab the attention of your audience quicker than just text. Humans are visual beings. When putting your research into practice and creating marketing materials, aesthetics are important.

Multimedia content, such as photography and videography, can often tell a story better than words. You can evoke emotions, create desire, and build trust simply by using a well-placed and well-created video, photo, or graphic. Although quality copywriting can be persuasive, some well-placed visual content can take it a step further.

With a product launch, in particular, potential customers need to have every question answered about the product before the actual launch. The more visual information and answers they have, the more likely you will be to convert interest into sales. You can lead a potential customer to your product online, but unless it looks alluring and what they see confirms how they feel about their need for your product, you risk losing the sale at the most critical time.

I'm asked about this a lot by entrepreneurs looking to get started on their journey: "Do I need a product video?" "How many photos should I have?" "When does my brand need a logo and brand identity information?" At this early stage in your journey, you don't need an entire library of photography, brand videos, and Apple-level web graphics. You can make do with just the fundamentals.

Here are recommendations on the types of content to consider creating for validation:

- Product photography (or photo-realistic renders)
  - Generally shot in a studio environment
  - Dark background versus light background versus color backgrounds
  - 6 to 12 photos/photorealistic renders

- Lifestyle photography
  - Generally shot in locations/environments relevant to how the product will be used by a customer
  - Demographics of models (if you're using models, consider their age, gender, attire, etc., given your target audience)
  - 6 to 12 photos

- Behind-the-scenes photography (design, production, team)
  - Could be as simple as headshots or selfies taken in a workshop or office
  - 6 to 12 photos

- Videography
  - Ideally, a short video clip, GIF, or stop-motion video can be created to give some interactivity to your early marketing content
  - Things to consider including in a video:
    - The Problem -> The key pain point your customers experience that your idea solves

- Our Solution -> A presentation of your idea/solution
- Product Features and Specs -> Key elements of the product
- Product Benefits -> What the product enables you to do or feel
- How It Works -> Step-by-step user journey
- Credibility and Awards -> What users and experts are saying
- Founders Intro -> Why we're crowdfunding, call-to-action
  - Any video should include occasional subtitles and layover text so that it's understandable to people who view it with the sound turned off or those who have hearing difficulties.

This list will be more than sufficient for any early validation testing. In fact, one could even argue that the videography is surplus. A core objective of the Five-Step High-Profit Launch System is to keep it low risk and low cost. If, for you, that means focusing only on photos or photorealistic renders for now and considering video a nice-to-have, then so be it. While video is valuable content to have, many successful validations have been run without it.

Validation: Simple Tests to Get a Green or Red Light

Remember, all this work on audiences, branding, and messaging is to serve one core purpose: determining if you should or shouldn't launch your business. It's not about knowing exactly who your target customer is or the best image to use in an ad (keep reading to Chapters 4 and 5 for that); it's about knowing if people will want what you're offering. You can use these validation tests to answer other questions, such as: "Would this product sell better as a subscription or a one-off payment?" and "Would it be more profitable to sell two in a bundle package?" You must answer the most critical question first, though: "Will people be interested in buying this product at the price I want to sell it?" Don't get bogged down in the details (yet).

You can determine the answer to this key question, without much time or money, by conducting a few tests with your target audiences. The key is to minimize the variables in these tests, such as the price of your product or the specific target audience you are testing. A lot of people ask me: "Can we test a million things?" I have to explain that, no, you must focus on your high-priority variables in order to collect meaningful data. More variables = more time and more money to collect the necessary information from the audience. Consider the variables that would be most impactful for your business and focus on those. Don't worry about testing everything (yet).

The tests themselves take the form of a simple sales funnel—the journey that a potential customer has to take in order to buy your product.

1. You show your target audience a marketing message →
2. Those who are interested click through to a page where you show them a specific offer →
3. Those who take you up on your offer receive confirmation of their interest, such as a welcome email or a pop-up message saying thank you

A big question we get from many folks is why go through this to determine if there's a market for your idea, when you could just ask your family, friends, or professional network?

The truth: there's nowhere you'll get more brutal honesty than from keyboard warriors hidden behind a screen. Your mom, best friend, or work colleague won't tell you that your idea sucks. Someone 3,000 miles away who saw your ad on Facebook will, without hesitation. Likewise, if your idea is brilliant, you can be confident that a stranger is telling the truth, uncolored by your being their child, friend, or partner.

At each step of this test, you'll receive valuable data about the number of people interested in your idea. In addition to the numbers, you'll also be able to hear directly from your target audiences through people commenting on your ads or messaging you directly. The more impactful an offer, the more you'll hear from your audiences. "Oh my gosh, I NEED this," or "$149? Are you insane? That's way too much."

Let's break down two popular validation blueprints online merchants can use today: the 1 Percent Funnel and the Fake Checkout.

The 1 Percent Funnel

To start the funnel, you show your target audience a marketing message

- Run ads via Facebook/Instagram that show your product and the solution it offers to the user. Think of it as a simple introduction. For example, an ad we used for a coffee-maker client we helped to launch was: "COFFEEJACK™ is the world's smallest espresso machine. No electricity, pods, or filters. Just great coffee."

Those who show interest are shown a specific offer

- Those who click on an ad (show interest) are taken to a web page (which you can set up easily with landing page platforms such as Unbounce, ClickFunnels, or KickOff Labs) where they have the option to sign up by submitting their email address to access deals when your product launches, such as: "Sign up to access discounts when we launch."

- Those who sign up are taken to a second web page, where you give them the option to pay 1 percent of the launch price and get guaranteed access to the biggest launch discount. For example: "Our best deals will run out quickly! Put 1 percent down now and *guarantee* 50 percent off when we launch."

Those who take up the offer receive confirmation of their interest

- All users who sign up on the first page receive a welcome message (often via email) that may ask them to complete an action. For example: "Confirm your email address."
- All users who put 1 percent down will then be taken to a third web page (as well as receive a welcome message) that may incentivize them to perform another action. For example: "Complete a survey for an additional 5 percent off."

From the audience's standpoint they go through this entire funnel in a maximum of six clicks of their mouse or taps on their screen. There's a lot going on under the surface, however, and this quick journey for the user has provided you, the creator, with invaluable information.

Let's look at another validation test blueprint: the Fake Checkout. This is a test we ran with Tula Mics, a microphone company that this system helped to raise $400,000 in four weeks.

The Fake Checkout

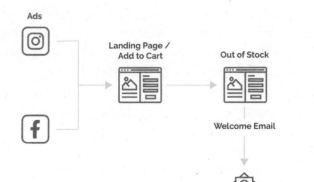

To start the funnel, show your target audience a marketing message

- Run ads via Facebook/Instagram that show your product and the solution it offers to the user.

Those who show interest are shown a specific offer

- Those who click on an ad are taken to a web page, where they have the option to buy the product (for example, "Buy Now" or "Add To Cart" buttons). Don't worry, you don't need to have the product ready yet.
- Those who attempt to buy are moved to a second web page, where they see a message indicating the product is out of stock, but they are given the option to provide their email address and to be notified when it becomes available again.

Those who take up the offer receive confirmation of their interest

- All users who provide their email address receive a welcome message that may ask them to complete an action. For example: "Confirm your email address" or "Complete a survey."

This test takes the user even fewer clicks or taps than the previous example. Just four!

At the conclusion of both of these tests, you'll have collected valuable information on the five following key components of launching your business:

1. How much it will cost to reach your target audiences through the advertising channels used in your tests
2. What percentage of people within your expected target audiences show interest in your idea (via the click-through rate of the ads)
3. What percentage of people show strong enough interest in your idea that they're considering buying it (via signing up on the first web page in the 1 Percent Funnel, or via the click-through rate of the "Buy Now" or "Add to Cart" buttons in the Fake Checkout)
4. What percentage of people are ready to buy your idea today (via making a 1 percent payment in the 1 Percent Funnel or signing up on the second "out of stock" page in the Fake Checkout Funnel)
5. How engaged your prospective customers are (how many people open the welcome message, complete the survey, or both)

These two validation test blueprints work for most online business ideas, but they won't necessarily work for everyone. Their underlying concept and goal, however, will. Regardless of what your validation tests look like, acquire evidence that enough people will buy whatever it is you're selling *before* you invest your hard-earned time and money in a comprehensive launch.

Red Flag Metrics: Pricing, Positioning, and Profit Margins

The main question you're looking to answer during validation is: will people be interested in buying this product idea? Within that larger question, there are three sub-questions that you are also seeking answers to through your validation tests:

1. Am I pricing the product idea appropriately?
2. Is the language and creative material (such as copy, photos, and videos) resonating with the target audiences?
3. Is the cost of selling the product idea appropriate for the business to be successful and sustainable?

Data suggesting the answer to any one of these questions is no are what you should look out for as Red Flag Metrics—numbers in your results that suggest your offer is going to face an uphill battle if you were to pursue it as a business.

1. Am I pricing the product idea appropriately?

In most cases, you've decided your pricing through market research, the cost of manufacturing, or a bit of both. By testing this pricing directly with your target audiences before you launch, you'll learn whether people bite your hand off to take advantage of it, or don't consider it worth the cost.

To answer this question, the main number you're looking for is your conversion rate. In the case of these funnels, this number is the percentage of people who click through your first ad, and on seeing the price of your idea, add their name to your sign-up list, put money down, or both. If lots of people click through your first ad, but no one signs up or puts money down, this is a Red Flag Metric, and it means either your price is too high, or that you perceive your product as a better solution than your potential customers do.

Alternatively, you may learn that your price is too low. One client I worked with learned that they had room to increase their price before launch. The percentage of people signing up and putting money down was very high, almost 15 percent (roughly double what we would usually hope to see for a product like theirs). They raised their prices and earned an extra 10 percent in revenue at launch with this one simple switch.

2. Is the language and creative material (such as copy, photos, and videos) resonating with the target audiences?

The testing period offers a high-level look at which messages, audiences, and materials have the highest potential. Does one of your ads resonate better than another? Is one key feature of your idea much more exciting to folks than another? What should your product name be?

As you'll recall from earlier in the chapter, during your validation period, you'll test three to four audiences, and a similar number of unique selling propositions (USPs). Once you've run your tests, you'll be able to point to which of these were the most successful. If one particular audience and USP performs very well (for example, people sign up and put money down three times more often than for your other audiences and USPs), you'll know to focus on that audience and that selling proposition when you launch. You'll know not to spend your money and time on the poorer performers, just the one that gets you the best results.

3. Is the cost of selling the product idea appropriate for the business to be successful and sustainable?

You might have a slam dunk product. That doesn't mean the strategy you were planning to use to launch it is also a slam dunk.

For example, if you want to be profitable right out of the gate and have a low-priced offer, e-commerce advertising in its current form will not work for you. At the time of this writing, the cost to reach your target audience through these channels is simply too high compared to the amount of revenue the customers you acquire from these funnels will generate. Often, the cost to advertise via social media and search engines remains relatively static, whether you're selling a $1 product or a $1,000 product. This makes selling low-priced products (profitably) impossible.

It's important to note, however, that a low-priced offer and a low-priced product are not the same thing. If your business is offering low-priced items, you can use bulk orders, product bundles, subscription models, upgrades, and additional accessories as ways to increase the average order value per customer and create a higher-priced offer. All online entrepreneurs should target an average order value of $100 or more. This gives you a good chance of profitability, even when using paid marketing methods like Facebook ads. Sure, you can make up for a low price with smart advertising and keeping your other costs low, but only up to a point. If you price your offer too low, there is simply no way to make up for it with online sales. This is a harsh reality of doing business online.

With what you learn about pricing and the cost of advertising during this early validation period, you can start to make accurate predictions of what your profit margins will be down the line. This is vital for the short- and long-term success of your business. I've seen entrepreneurs who had many people interested in their offer, but who lost money on every sale when they launched, all because they didn't account for the cost of marketing when determining the price of their product.

Passing the Go/No-Go Test

Ultimately, the goal of this stage is to determine if you should or shouldn't pursue your business. Yet, as you've learned, there are a lot of questions that go into this determination, each with their own set of benchmark numbers. Once you've run your tests, it can be hard to decipher your findings. Here is a basic rundown of what your data will look like (roughly) from each of the two tests in this chapter, if you've confirmed there is a market for your idea, and the cost of selling to that market is sustainable. In short, here's what a "Go" verdict looks like.

For the 1 Percent Funnel example:

- CPM (cost per thousand advertising impressions): <$20 (the cost it takes to display your ads to users)
- Ad Landing Page Sign up: >20 percent (the percentage of visitors to your web page that sign up to hear more about your offer, demonstrating interest)
- 1 Percent Purchase Completion: >5 percent (the percentage of web page sign-ups who then also make a 1 percent payment)
- 1 Percent Purchase Completion Cost Per Action: <30 percent of the product offer price (the average amount you spend on advertising to acquire a 1 percent purchase)
- Welcome Email Open Rate: >50 percent (the percentage of sign-ups who open your first marketing email)

For the Fake Checkout example:

- CPM (cost per thousand advertising impressions): <$20 (the cost it takes to display your ads to users)
- "Buy Now" or "Add to Cart" button clicks: >40 percent (the percentage of web visitors who try to purchase your offer, showing purchase intent)

- "Out of Stock" Web Page Sign-Up Cost Per Lead: <$5 (the average amount you spend on advertising to acquire a sign-up on this page)
- Welcome Email Open Rate: >50 percent (the percentage of sign-ups who open your first marketing email)

Remember, the information here is not prescriptive and rigid! If you end up with a CPM at $21 rather than sub $20, that's okay. Each validation has its own nuances. The numbers outlined above are general rules of thumb that can set you up for success.

With real data in hand, you can now start making realistic projections on the success of your launch. This can help you answer important questions, such as:

- How big of a community will need to be built to reach the launch goals?
- How much marketing spend will be required to acquire a customer?
- What will the return on investment be?

Let's consider some equations you can plug your 1 Percent Funnel validation data into that will allow you to predict future success and look at an example. Review these now, but you'll also likely want to revisit them several times as you make your way through the book and during your launch marketing efforts.

Pre-Launch Marketing Predictions

1. *Pre-Launch Advertising Budget / Cost per Landing Page Sign-Up = Size of Launch Community*
2. *(Number of 1 Percent Reservations Acquired in Validation / Size of Validation Community) x 100 = Customer Conversion Rate*

3. *Customer Conversion Rate x Size of Your Launch Community = Early Launch Customers*
4. *Early Launch Customers x Price of Your Product = Early Launch Revenue*
5. *Pre-Launch Advertising Spend / Early Launch Customers = Early Launch Customer Acquisition Cost*
6. *Early Launch Revenue / Pre-Launch Advertising Budget = Return on Pre-Launch Investment*

Example of a product launch with a $199 price point and a $5,000 pre-launch advertising budget:

1. $5,000 pre-launch advertising budget / $2 per sign-up = 2,500 members of a launch community
2. (20 / 500) x 100 = 4 percent conversion rate
3. 4 percent x 2,500 = 100 early launch customers
4. 100 x $199 = $19,900 early launch revenue
5. $5,000 / 100 = $50 early launch customer acquisition cost
6. $19,900 / $5,000 = 3.98x return on investment

Post-Launch Marketing Predictions

1. *Pre-Launch Ad Spend per 1 Percent Reservation x 125* percent *= Post-Launch Customer Acquisition Cost*
2. *(Price of Your Product / Pre-Launch Ad Spend per 1 Percent Reservation) x Advertising Budget = Additional Launch Revenue*
3. *Total Launch Revenue / Spend = Return On Investment*
4. *Total Launch Revenue / Price of Your Product = Total Number of Customers*

Example of that same product launch as it continues into the launch day and post-launch sales period, with a $199 price point and a $5,000 post-launch advertising budget:

1. $50 x 1.25x = $62.50 post-launch customer acquisition cost
2. ($199 / $62.50) x $5,000 = $15,920 post-launch revenue
3. ($19,900 + $15,920) / $10,000 = 3.58x return on investment
4. ($19,900 + $15,920) / $199 = 180 launch customers

In this particular product launch scenario, the entrepreneur can plug in his or her own validation data and predict they would generate an overall 3.58x return on their investment from 180 launch customers. If they look at these numbers and decide they want more launch revenue, they can simply plug in higher advertising budgets. If they see a 3.58x return on investment and conclude that's not enough given their potential production costs, they know they need to improve their conversion rate or increase their price point in order to increase the revenue they will achieve from their advertising spend.

These aren't perfect or exact equations. There is no one-size-fits-all. Yet what analysis like this can give any entrepreneur is more information. This, in turn, gives them the knowledge to assess and reduce their future risk.

Pump the Gas or Pivot?

At the conclusion of a validation, we always want the data to look good. If there are no red flags and metrics hit benchmarks, it's time to pump the gas.

Unfortunately, the reality is that there are times when the data does *not* look good. This leaves an entrepreneur with a decision: pump the gas (and take a humongous risk) or pivot. Pivot could mean scrapping an idea entirely and moving onto the next one. It could also mean pivoting the existing idea to make it more appealing to the target market.

Eric Ries, author of *The Lean Startup,* suggests that there are 10 types of pivots entrepreneurs can make during this early stage of validating an idea. I'm going to focus on the three that I see the most:

1. **Zoom-in pivot.** Many entrepreneurs during validation will see one feature or use case of their product getting far more traction and interest than the others. They can then pivot by offering a new product that offers only that one feature or focuses on that one use case.

2. **Customer segment pivot.** Your product idea may prove popular but not with the audience segment that you had initially targeted. Look for these pockets of opportunity in your validation data, as you'll often see certain audiences outperform your broader target audience. With this kind of pivot, your USP, pricing/business model, messaging, and channels would all need to be reviewed.

3. **Value capture pivot.** This pivot refers to changes involving how you generate revenue. Oftentimes, entrepreneurs might see a product idea positioned with one particular pricing fail a validation test, while a relatively small change in their pricing then leads to success. For example, switching from a one-off payment to a subscription model or bundling products together.

Grandy's Glorious Bakery

Throughout this book, I'll be walking through each step of the Five-Step High-Profit Launch System with an imaginary business to demonstrate how these concepts translate into practical steps you can take for your idea.

Allow me to introduce you to Grandy and her business idea, Grandy's Glorious Bakery. Grandy, my mum's mum, baked the most phenomenal cakes. Every time we visited when I was a child, like Pavlov's dogs, my stomach would start rumbling as we pulled into the driveway. After the 90-minute drive south from our home in the suburbs of London, Grandy would be waiting for us at the front door, an apron on and a rolling pin often in her hand. Cakes, cookies, flapjacks, pastries, pies—you name it, she made it. I can't think of a better person to go through the Five-Step High-Profit Launch System.

One day, after eating a particularly delicious cookie, I told Grandy that her baking was so good, she should share it beyond her immediate family. "Let's start selling these to your neighbors and the local community," I suggested.

"Oh, no, my love," Grandy said, "I don't think anyone would be interested in little old me."

Before sending Grandpa off to the supermarket to buy massive amounts of ingredients and setting Grandy to work, we first wanted to validate that people would, in fact, be interested in buying from her not-yet-existent business, Grandy's Glorious Bakery. Here's how we did it:

1. We set up a simple web page introducing the business, showcasing five of our favorite Grandy bakes, and presenting a launch discount for our first customers. If a potential customer signed up on the page, we gave them a 30 percent discount code.

2. To drive folks to this page, we set up two traffic sources.

    First, we purchased Facebook ads. Using a $100 budget, we targeted anyone in a 25-mile radius with an interest in baking, bakeries, cakes, baking TV shows, and cookies.

    Second, we put up a poster at Grandpa's local golf club, highlighting the 30 percent discount and the link to Grandy's web page. We also added a phone number, so those who were less internet savvy could call up and we could enter their name to claim their early customer discount from our end.

3. When they signed up, we sent them a second offer via email, asking them to "start" their order by taking a short survey asking which baked good (cake, pie, or cookie) they were most interested in and how many they wanted. (This is another version of the 1 Percent Funnel or the Fake Checkout we mentioned earlier in the chapter.) If they took this survey, we promised to include a free cookie with their order.

After a week, we reviewed the numbers. How many people visited the website? How many called us? How many signed up for a discount? How many "started" their order? We saw that from 200 visits to the page, 70 had signed up for the discount, 50 had started their order, and the average value of those orders was $25 (accounting for the 30 percent discount). If all 50 people completed their purchase, Grandy would make $1,250. Even if only 25 went on to complete their purchase, she would still make $625.

The key Red Flag Metric for Grandy was how much money she could make per hour by making her baking more than just a hobby. If she would take home less than, let's say, $40 per hour, she decided she'd prefer to be relaxing and reading in her retirement years, rather than toiling away in a kitchen.

For this reason, we needed to understand her costs as well as her revenue. Her expenses included $100 in advertising and the $50 she predicted the ingredients for 25 orders would cost (totaling $150). She thought it would take her four hours to bake those orders, and one more hour to deliver them. With $625 in revenue and $150 in expenses, she would therefore earn $475. This equates to $95 per hour for those five hours of work. Well above what she would consider a Red Flag and not bad at all for a retiree!

After running the go/no-go test and finding favorable results, Grandy was onboard and ready to get baking!

My Favorite Tools

At the end of each chapter in which we go through a particular step of the Five-Step High-Profit Launch System, I'll be sharing with you my favorite tools for completing this step on your own.

During the validation step, you'll find me using:

- **Unbounce:** Landing page builder for us to design, develop, test, and optimize launch marketing web pages.
- **Facebook/Instagram Advertising:** My go-to marketing channel for promoting an offer to potential customers and driving them to our landing pages.
- **Stripe:** Payment processor to collect 1 percent reservations.
- **Klaviyo:** Email marketing and SMS marketing platform, where we can collect and communicate with our email and SMS communities.
- **Google Forms:** Simple survey tool to collect answers from prospective customers.
- **Google Analytics:** Analytics platform that allows us to evaluate the behavior and performance of our web traffic.
- **Hotjar Analytics:** Analytics platform that allows us to evaluate the behavior and experience of our web traffic.
- **Databox:** Analytics dashboard that allows us to collate marketing from different platforms in one, clean view.
- **Adobe Creative Suite:** Software we use for graphic design, video editing, web development, and photography.
- **Google Drive:** My go-to file storage platform where we keep any and every document, PowerPoint, graphic, analysis, and folder created during a launch.

CHAPTER FOUR

Find Your First Supporters

I N THIS CHAPTER, you'll learn about Audience Acquisition, Step 2 of the Five-Step High-Profit Launch System, including:

- The decision-making process of your target audience
- Tricks and tips from advanced marketers on persuasion
- Different funnels (customer journeys) to consider for your launch
- How to minimize risk by creating multiple audience touchpoints
- Kicking off your viral growth generators

This should be done after you have validated your idea and proven it has real potential. It is recommended you allow yourself one to two months to complete the strategies in this chapter.

What Makes People Want Stuff?

If you've validated your idea and determined that it can indeed become a successful business, great! You've avoided the biggest mistake among early entrepreneurs—not confirming that their idea is something the market wants. Now, we quickly move to avoid the second biggest mistake: failing to build an audience around your idea *before* you launch your business.

I've seen it many times: an entrepreneur spends countless long days and late nights creating a great product. As their launch date nears, their anxiety level goes sky high. They have butterflies that keep them from eating and fears of failure that keep them from sleeping. Launch day finally arrives. This is the day they've been waiting for, working toward, the day to which all their blood, sweat, and tears have led. All engines are running, the website is live, here we go! And—crickets. Nada. Zilch. They built it but no one came. A nightmare scenario that every entrepreneur fears.

As the hours tick by and the entrepreneur sees no one visiting their site or talking about their business online, and no sales coming in, a feeling of failure cuts at them like a knife to their gut. They struggle to comprehend how all of their hard work has resulted in silence. No one cares. It's one of the worst feelings a new entrepreneur can experience. They validated the idea; people want the product! Why has this happened?

It's simple—they failed to create a community of potential customers before the launch!

If you plan to launch an idea that will change the world, you first have to build excitement about it. Like ripples in a pond, you have to drop a pebble into the water to stimulate the wave motion. The community of potential customers you build before your launch is that pebble: small but mighty, and essential in giving your idea the energy to spread. You should acquire such a community weeks or months before launch day itself. This could be an email list, a private online or in-person community, or any other type of group of people who support your idea.

In order to build this community, you first need to understand what it is about your idea that people like and expand upon it. You must ask yourself the fundamental question: what makes people want (your) stuff?

In 2001, shortly before Apple launched the iPod, they broadcast one of the most well-known taglines of all time: "1,000 songs in your pocket." This is a perfect example of how to make people want stuff. In this simple line, Apple highlights the benefit to a potential buyer and generates an emotional reaction, rather than showcasing the specifics of the offer itself. The average consumer didn't care about the iPod's processor speed, the RAM, or the connectivity. They cared that this little device could give them a large library of music, anywhere and anytime.

At the most basic level, people want stuff for one of two reasons: to move closer to pleasure, or farther away from pain. They don't want stuff because of the stuff itself, but how the stuff makes them feel. The pleasure it brings them toward, or the pain it takes them away from.

One facet of this is socialization. Why do people stand in lines for hours outside movie theatres to see blockbuster films? Why do people say: "Never eat at an empty restaurant?" Seeing that other people want something makes us more likely to want it too. Vice-versa, if others around us do not appear to want something, we're less likely to want it.

Another tool at your disposal is scarcity. It is a natural human response to panic when resources are scarce, and savvy entrepreneurs know to take advantage of that. This is why tactics like limited availability (time or quantity) work so well. They tap into the innate human fear of missing out, making customers more likely to take immediate action—to want whatever the marketer is selling even more!

I went to Brazil in 2014 for the men's soccer World Cup. The tickets made available from FIFA for the games were very limited in quantity and could be acquired on a first-come, first-served basis. On a particular date, tickets were made available online and once the limited number were purchased, that was it. The only option would then be to try to buy a ticket from someone else at a ludicrous markup (which, itself, is a classic example of how social proof—demand—makes something more valuable).

The scarcity of the tickets resulted in me waking up at 4 am, accessing the FIFA website through four different devices and refreshing all four constantly in order to make sure at least one of those devices managed to get into the booking engine and complete a purchase before tickets were sold out.

As anticipated, tickets were gone in minutes. My early morning and fast work did indeed allow me to get my hands on a ticket for a game at the tournament (Argentina vs. Belgium, for those interested—an opportunity for me to see Lionel Messi in action and at his peak).

In fact, people can even be made to want stuff that doesn't actually exist. It's all about the launch marketing system going on behind the scenes. In 2015, Cards Against Humanity famously asked their customers to give them money ($5) for absolutely nothing in return. Incredibly, the card game-maker reeled in $71,145 from 11,248 people who gave $5 or more.

Employees ended up splitting the profits and using the money for everything from game consoles, cars, down payments, college tuition, whiskey, plane tickets to Finland, mattresses, and donations to a variety of charities. That's the power of an effective launch marketing system.

What can we learn from this?

People often want stuff not because of what that stuff is or does, but how that stuff makes them feel.

Why on earth did 11,248 buyers give money for absolutely nothing in return? I would argue it made them feel unique. It was an act of rebellion to match the marketing campaign—one which mocks the world of consumerism that most of us are swallowed up by on a daily, hourly basis. Participating alongside Cards Against Humanity in this ironic, "anti-marketing" marketing campaign made them feel special, acknowledged, and was a reflection on how they wanted others to see them.

You might not have the personal creativity or brand credibility to pull a stunt like Cards Against Humanity, but you can certainly pursue marketing efforts with the perspective of making your customers and community feel unique, included, and understood.

The Buyer Decision Process

Don't be misled by the term "buyer" to be one solely related to finances. While some buyer decisions have more of a financial essence, you buy into any decision regardless of whether it's a monetary one or not. You make a buyer decision when you decide what to do with your Saturday afternoon or when you choose a new book to read from your bookshelf.

The five stages of the buyer decision process were first introduced by John Dewey in 1910 and are as follows:

1. Problem/Need Recognition - Recognizing the problem or need and identifying the solution that is required.
2. Information Search - Researching the solution that would satisfy the need.
3. Evaluation of Alternatives - Generally, the information search reveals a few different solutions to evaluate and understand which would be most appropriate.
4. Buyer Decision - After the buyer has evaluated all the options and any solvable objections are resolved, they're ready to make the decision.
5. Post-Decision Behavior - After the decision, the buyer may experience post-purchase dissonance feeling that another solution would have been better, or they may feel reinforcement that they made the correct decision and may go on to advocate that decision to others.

Most significant for this book is the time needed for this buyer decision process, which will differ for each stage. The effort devoted to each stage depends on a number of factors, such as the perceived risk of the decision (e.g., a product's price) and the consumer's motivations (e.g., an impulsive personal choice versus a decision for your family). For some decisions, it takes a fraction of a second and most of the decision process is unconscious. For others, the process might take years.

In the case of an impulse purchase or a decision that requires low risk, the buyer will likely spend minimal time engaged in information search and evaluation and proceed directly to the actual purchase. Need recognition may not even be a conscious realization. An example of this might be a user scrolling through Instagram, seeing an ad, clicking through, and buying the product in the ad immediately.

In a case where the decision is high-risk and requires a higher burden of decision-making, there may be many decision-makers involved and each step of the process is conscious and thorough. An example of this could be buying a car or a house. Information search and evaluation might take a considerable amount of time in such decisions, as you consider the financial implications, research many different options, and often involve more than one person in making that final decision.

Let's reflect on the copywriting formula we discussed previously to see how a buyer decision process can be integrated into a launch marketing strategy. Remember our formula, the Five Rule Recipe:

| HIGHLIGHT THE PAIN POINT | HIGHLIGHT THE DREAM | MAKE A PROMISE | SHOW PROOF | ASK FOR ACTION |

Now, let's consider how you could align this with the buyer decision process. And let's use a real example, perhaps the buyer decision process for a new set of earbuds:

1. **Problem/Need Recognition <-> Highlight the pain point.** Some people will know they're in need of new earbuds; perhaps they lost theirs or one has stopped playing audio. Others, though, may not recognize the need or understand an offer as the solution until it's made clear to them. These new earbuds are noise-canceling, unlike the buyer's current pair. Until they saw a promotional video, they hadn't realized just how much recent earbud technology can limit background noise. Great, their interest has been piqued!

2. **Information Search <-> Highlight the dream.** They've been wowed by the technology of noise-canceling; now they're digging a little deeper: How much will this cost them? What else do these new earbuds offer that their current pair doesn't? Does their current pair have anything that these new ones don't? Ensuring the marketing for this new product clearly showcases the benefits, the value, and how they will make the buyer feel will be key during this stage. An example of this we've all seen many times in marketing could be a promotional video presenting this transition from pain to delight. For example, it could show a woman getting onto a busy subway train, the noisy clanging of the train on the tracks and people talking all around them. It's been raining and she doesn't have an umbrella, so she's wet. She's also running late, having to sprint to catch the train and only just making it into the carriage before the doors close. Her day is not going to plan, she's frazzled and frustrated, so the color in the video is tinted and dark to represent this emotional state. Then, she puts the earbuds in. The noise stops. The colors brighten. You see her select a playlist of her favorite songs and press play. She smiles and, in an instant, everything is good again.

3. **Evaluation of Alternatives <-> Make a promise.** Now the buyer has been made aware of the core USP, noise-canceling functionality, it's time to consider what other products offer it. Are there better alternatives? At this stage, it's the responsibility of the marketer to prove that their marketing claims are legitimate and that this solution is, indeed, better than anything else available on the market. Put your stake in the ground and your name on the line: this is the solution for them. There are no other earbuds that can compete.

4. **Buyer Decision <-> Make a promise/show proof/ask for action.** As a buyer closes on the decision, it's the responsibility of the marketer to reduce the risk of the decision the buyer is about to make. Displaying other buyer reviews (think Amazon, Google,

or Facebook reviews) and offer guarantees (like money-back or warranties) are marketing tactics you can use to give the buyer confidence in their decision and help nudge them across the finish line. If the buyer loves what the new earbuds appear to offer, can see that previous buyers were happy in their buying decision, and also have a guarantee from the seller that they receive a refund if they're unhappy, what more can they ask for to make their buying decision a safe bet? Just like entrepreneurs, consumers, too, are seeking ways to minimize their risk.

5. **Post Decision Behavior <-> Ask for action.** Marketing efforts don't end with the buyer's decision. Post-purchasing strategies can be used to both improve the current solution (collecting customer feedback) as well as increase proof (asking for customer reviews).

When launching a product, you can tell such a story in many ways. The above narrative can be translated into a web page, an email sequence, a brochure, a sales deck, or a product video. It could be for a pitch, a call script, an essay, or an ad. For a pair of earbuds, this whole story might be told on an Amazon page. If you're buying a house, it might be told across months of meetings, tours, brochures, emails, calls, and negotiations.

Be careful not to get too caught up in the complexities and remember one thing: people want stuff not because of what that stuff is or does, but how that stuff makes them feel.

One Touch Isn't Enough

Have you ever been told not to put all your eggs in one basket? If you've ever spoken to me, or someone as risk averse as I am, the answer is surely: yes. This phrase was said to be first used in the novel *Don Quixote*, where it was written: "It is the part of a wise man to keep himself today for tomorrow, and not venture all his eggs in one basket."

Putting all your efforts and resources in one area (eggs in one basket) is the epitome of risk. One mistake and you could lose everything. In the philosophy of risk aversion, it is recommended you put eggs in as many different baskets as possible.

In launch marketing terms, this is a common issue. Oftentimes, those launching new ideas rely almost exclusively on one method of communication to speak with prospective buyers. Consider email marketing, for example. Many entrepreneurs, particularly in a product launch arena such as crowdfunding, commit a lot of resources to building an email list of subscribers before they launch. This will allow them to send an email to these potential buyers when a product becomes available, with the intention of driving a lot of traction and sales right from the moment of launch.

While this is often a solid route to go and can go off without a hitch, there's no plan B. Risk-aversion is all about considering the "what ifs" and having not just a plan B, but a C, D, and E.

A few years ago, I was working on the launch of a technology eyewear product. There was a lot of interest in the product, people were excited to get their hands on a pair, and we had prioritized one core marketing communication channel for these folks: email marketing.

Two days before launch, disaster struck.

In our final pre-launch email to the subscriber list, we noticed the open rate of our email sends plummeted from something like a 50 percent open rate down to a mere 10 percent. All of a sudden, almost no one was opening the emails we were sending.

These days, the launch system has a pretty tight process if this were to happen (a file aptly named in our task management system as: Email Marketing Emergency Actions). Back then, this was a first for us.

After hours of digging, we discovered that the domain we were using in the sender name of our emails (e.g., the "myimaginarycompany.com" piece of the sender name "johnsmith@myimaginarycompany.com") had been blacklisted by the email providers (Gmail, Yahoo Mail, Outlook, and so on) due to website security errors on the client's part, and this had then been flagged by the email platform (the mass email tool we were using to send emails to thousands of prospective buyers). This meant that emails being sent were being pushed into spam folders rather than inboxes. While you can always expect some emails to go into spam folders, it should never be the significant majority!

We were in trouble. No matter how excited or interested these potential buyers were, if we couldn't place an email in their inboxes on launch day, then we had no way of informing them the product was now available. Thousands of excited community members would be left in the dark, unaware that our preorder sale was kicking off.

In the end, we were able to somewhat save the situation by employing workaround tactics to reach these email subscribers via different marketing channels. It was far from a perfect solution, though, and significantly impacted the success of the launch.

Lesson learned: one touch (one method of communication with community members) was not enough. Never again would I be putting all my eggs in one basket.

It was from this lesson that the launch system and funnels within it were adapted to create as many touch points as possible.

In the previous chapter, we looked at a 1 Percent Funnel:

How many touch points (methods of communication) with a potential buyer can you see there? In other words, once a potential buyer has completed their journey through the funnel, how many different ways could you get in touch with him or her in the future?

For me, there's only really one: email. In this journey through the funnel, a potential buyer has provided you with their email address.

You can therefore contact them via email in the future. If your answer includes other possible touch points, such as retargeting audiences or a suggestion that the 1 percent transaction may somehow provide a touch point, you're not wrong. However, I wouldn't consider such communication methods as *core* touch points, so we'll put them aside for now.

Now, consider a more advanced 1 Percent Funnel:

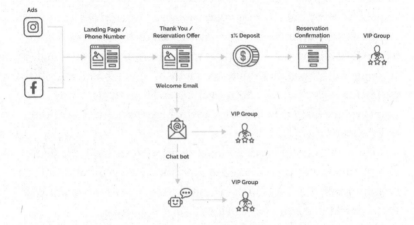

This is a 1 Percent Funnel you might run after you've validated your product or idea, and your focus can move from proving market fit to preparing for launch. In addition to the deposit ask, this funnel prioritizes creating multiple touch points quickly and easily.

How many touch points with a potential buyer can you see in this expanded funnel?

Like before, we've got email. We've also got an opportunity for an SMS/phone number touch point, a Facebook Messenger chat bot touch point, as well as multiple opportunities for a VIP Group touch point. If someone moves through this funnel and takes the actions asked of them, we would then have four touch points with them rather than just one. Eggs in four baskets, not one. And, from a timing standpoint, this second, more advanced funnel really wouldn't feel much more complicated to the potential buyer. It would take a few clicks and a few seconds to move through, just like the simpler version.

That's particularly important, so I'll say it again: it would take only a few clicks and a few seconds for the potential customer, but it gives you four different ways to communicate with them.

Things should always be easy for the potential customer. Just like an iceberg, there's a lot going on underneath the surface with a multi-touch funnel like this, but the end customer doesn't have to know or deal with that. That's your burden to bear. Make it easy for the customer by: (a) allowing touch points to be created in the most simple way (for example, having someone add their phone number into a form field rather than asking them to text a number for entry) and (b) through the options most preferred by them (if you know your likely customers spend a lot of time on Facebook, for example, create touch points on that platform, such as Facebook Messenger, Facebook Events, or Facebook Groups).

Diversification of touch points also helps you achieve the perfect mix of sufficient communication to drive the action you want, without becoming overbearing. Too many messages in a short period of time via the same, single channel can lead to an unsubscribe.

When it comes to the number of prospect contacts necessary to guarantee success, there's plenty of evidence that suggests response rates in B2C (business to consumer) rise with each outreach attempt up to eight. If you contact a prospect less than eight times while they're making their purchasing decision, you're likely not fulfilling your idea's potential. Yet you don't want to be the annoying salesperson that won't leave the customer alone. You may have heard of ad blindness, also known as banner blindness or banner noise. This is where visitors to a website consciously or subconsciously ignore banner-like information like online ads. They become blind to it. Something similar can be said of launch marketing communications. For example, for every email a prospective buyer receives in your launch period, statistics show they're a little less likely to read it. This changes when you diversify those contact methods. Someone who receives an email one week, an SMS the following week, and communication through a Facebook

Group the week following, is often more likely to remain engaged than if they received an email each week.

There's a lot going on here, so let's take a look at a real-life funnel in which multiple touch points are collected:

Step 1: A web page requests a prospective buyer to add their name, email address (touchpoint one), and their phone number (touchpoint two).

Step 2: One click later, the prospect arrives at a page inviting them to join a private Facebook Group (touchpoint three).

Step 3: The email they receive after subscribing gives them a chance to prioritize communication through Facebook Messenger (touchpoint four).

Are you ready?

Confirm your 50% launch discount by answering one simple question:

How would you like to get notified when we launch?

PSST: Messenger subscribers get early access to the best discounts when we launch. (Up to 1 hour earlier than most!)

Notify me by Email

Notify me by Messenger

Thank you for that.

We'll keep you posted with more launch updates.

To a more productive you,

Step 4: The final stage of the journey offers the prospect an opportunity to start their order and share their feedback on the product, providing a deeper level of brand engagement and yet another touch point for prospect communication (touchpoint five).

In a handful of clicks and a matter of seconds, one prospective buyer could create five different touchpoints with the brand and your risk is reduced with this diversification of communication channels.

And the results speak for themselves. See an example of how different touchpoints performed in converting prospects into customers on product launches.

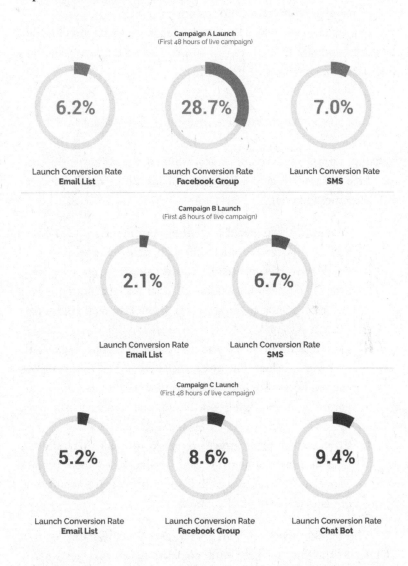

Campaign A Launch
(First 48 hours of live campaign)

6.2%

Launch Conversion Rate
Email List

28.7%

Launch Conversion Rate
Facebook Group

7.0%

Launch Conversion Rate
SMS

Campaign B Launch
(First 48 hours of live campaign)

2.1%

Launch Conversion Rate
Email List

6.7%

Launch Conversion Rate
SMS

Campaign C Launch
(First 48 hours of live campaign)

5.2%

Launch Conversion Rate
Email List

8.6%

Launch Conversion Rate
Facebook Group

9.4%

Launch Conversion Rate
Chat Bot

While these product launches saw perfectly adequate conversion rates of their email lists immediately after launch, hovering between

2 percent to 7 percent, they were far surpassed by the other touch-points. SMS lists gave a small boost, chat bot lists a further boost still, and a Facebook Group saw a tremendous increase with almost 30 percent of members converting into customers.

In a scenario whereby we'd relied on only one touchpoint for these launches—put all our eggs in one basket—we would have taken on a huge risk and missed a big opportunity.

Kicking Off Your Viral Growth Generators

When you think about customer acquisition in the online world, there are three key growth generators that will contribute to your success: paid, organic, and viral.

1. Paid acquisition means presenting your message to customers and acquiring customers through paid channels, such as Google advertising, Facebook advertising, or print advertising. This is the core acquisition channel for new entrepreneurs and new brands and a key piece of the Five-Step High-Profit Launch System.

2. Organic acquisition refers to acquisition that comes organically over time, such as blog posts, social media marketing, or web content becoming more visible online. Generally, this occurs naturally as you build your brand, and this isn't usually an option for folks who are just launching.

3. Viral acquisition is growth achieved through user referrals, such as someone sharing your product with their friends. Many launch strategies include some form of viral acquisition, pre-launch, post-launch, or both.

We'll dig into these different growth generators in more detail in Chapter 8. The third of these, viral acquisition, can be a particularly useful asset in your early launch marketing acquisition, particularly for entrepreneurs with very limited budgets, so it deserves its own small section here, too. In addition to driving valuable acquisition on its own, it can also trigger and speed-up organic acquisition—something sorely lacking for many new products and brands early on.

A simple example of a viral acquisition strategy for a launch would be a "refer-a-friend" campaign. This invites existing community members who already know your brand to share it with their friends and family, perhaps via their social networks or by email. Given that the information is being shared by a trusted source (friend of family), the recipients are more likely to sign up, too, and become a referred community member (rather than "paid").

To start, you need to clarify a few key pieces:

- **Determine your rewards.** What does someone receive for getting their friends or family to sign up? I like to go with reward tiers, starting with something small (an extra discount) for those who refer just one person, to higher-value rewards for community members who refer many (buy one, get one free). Be careful of offering too many freebies, though. Giving away free stuff can often result in freebie-seekers signing up for the program—not the audience you want in your community, as they're very unlikely to buy your product!
- **Choose when to ask community members to participate.** Is this refer-a-friend program the first thing they see after signing up? Does it get delivered by email later on? I like to place it early on in the funnel, perhaps in the welcome email. The earlier in the funnel, the more likely more people are to see it.
- **Design the experience.** Tracking referrals and building something like this on your own is hard. There are plenty of great tools you can use that are very user-friendly for getting this experience setup, such as KickOff Labs or ViralLoops.

The metric to focus on with viral acquisition is the viral coefficient: the number of new community members who are referred by one single community member. For example, a coefficient of 1.1 means that every new user who joins pulls in 1.1 new users on average. While 1 is

the magic number, there's value in launching marketing referral programs bringing in a lower viral coefficient. After all, launch marketing
involves different types of acquisition—you're not leaning entirely on
virality for success. (Or if you are, you shouldn't be!) Personally, I think
every little bit helps. If even 5 percent of your community members
refer at least 1 person to a pre-launch campaign, you're diversifying
your acquisition methods and bringing in new, prospective customers. The size of the community being invited to participate is growing
constantly, too, resulting in compounding user growth. Additionally,
those who do participate are often highly engaged advocates of your
brand and the precise community members you want to be engaging
and rewarding. What's more, once the program is set up, it becomes its
own growth generator with little management required (unlike paid
acquisition, which requires constant attention).

Grandy Finds Her First Supporters

In the case of Grandy's Glorious Bakery, once we'd proven there was a
market for her business, we needed to start building an audience and
excitement around her delicious treats. That way, when she started her
business, there would be a crowd of people, ready to buy. Here's how we
did it:

1. From our validation test, we saw that the poster in Grandpa's
    golf club brought in more "orders" than the Facebook ads we
    ran. This also cost less money, so we decided to double down
    on that as a way to spread the word. Over the next few weeks,
    Grandpa played a round of golf at all of the courses within a
    25-mile radius. Grandy tagged along, freshly baked pastries
    in hand, and offered the clubhouse staff a free taste of her
    delicacies if she could put a poster up for her new venture on
    the notice board. The staff was always happy to oblige. As word

spread, our Pre-launch Sign-up List of 70 potential customers (created for the validation test) quickly became 300.

2. We switched our web page to present a different offer. We'd already validated the idea; we didn't need any more not-yet-real orders—we needed to acquire an audience. To spread the word about Grandy's bakery launch to as many people as possible, we added a referral bonus. Those who referred three of their friends to the Grandy's Glorious Bakery Pre-launch Sign-up List would get 10 percent off their first order, in addition to the 30 percent launch discount. Everyone loves an extra discount. This little tactic took us from 300 to 500 potential customers on our list. Grandy was getting nervous! Baking for a family of five is one thing, but 500 is quite another.

3. We added a field to the sign-up form on our web page for interested individuals to leave their phone number, in addition to their name and email address. We saw that almost 40 percent of sign-ups were leaving their phone numbers, giving us a new touchpoint for hundreds of potential customers.

Things were going well and Grandy was getting excited. Who would've thought a few simple steps could lead to this? An excited community of potential customers, all eager to tuck in to Grandy's treats.

My Favorite Tools

During the Audience Acquisition step, you'll find me using:

- **Unbounce:** Landing page builder for us to design, develop, test, and optimize launch marketing web pages.
- **Facebook/Instagram Advertising:** My go-to marketing channel for promoting an offer to potential customers and driving them to our landing pages.
- **Google/YouTube Advertising:** A secondary marketing channel for driving web traffic, in addition to Facebook/Instagram advertising.
- **Stripe:** Payment processor to collect 1 percent reservations.
- **Klaviyo:** Email marketing and SMS marketing platform, where we can collect and communicate with our email and SMS communities.
- **Google Analytics:** Analytics platform that allows us to evaluate the behavior and performance of our web traffic.
- **Databox:** Analytics dashboard that allows us to collate marketing from different platforms in one, clean view.
- **Adobe Creative Suite:** Software we use for graphic design, video editing, web development, and photography.
- **Google Drive:** My go-to file storage platform where we keep any and every document, PowerPoint, graphic, analysis, and folder created during a launch.
- **KickOff Labs:** Sweepstakes platform that allows us to create and track viral referral programs.

CHAPTER FIVE

Make Them Want It

I N THIS CHAPTER, you'll learn about Audience Engagement, Step 3 of the Five-Step High-Profit Launch System, including:

- The team you want for optimal engagement success
- How to ensure prospective buyers are ready to act when launch day arrives
- Key objections you can expect to hear from your audience and how to resolve those objections before they arise
- That trust and honesty are the bedrock of launch success
- The role your community can play in driving excitement and action among others

This should be done concurrently with the previous chapter (Audience Acquisition), *after* you have validated your idea and proven it has real potential. In parallel with audience acquisition, it is recommended you allow yourself one to two months to complete the strategies in this chapter.

The Engagement Dream Team

Engaging with your potential first-ever customers is a big deal. Too many entrepreneurs skip this step, thinking the product itself is enough to convince people to make the purchase. When this step is skipped, the result is always the same—lower conversion rates of prospects into customers, lower revenue, and missed potential.

There are four key engagement roles I recommend you fill as you enter this stage of your journey (team members can play multiple roles):

1. **Community Manager:** The team member responsible for managing general communication and responding to questions. This could include social media or email post schedules, setting up new communities or events, responding to questions, comments, or concerns, and compiling resources for the community (such as an FAQ or how-to guide).

2. **Moderator(s):** As you get closer to your launch, things get hectic! The Community Manager may not be able to handle it alone. Quick responses to community member questions shows accountability, so adding a couple of additional Moderators to answer questions and respond to comments can help. This ensures all prospective customers have quick and seamless access to the brand team, building trust and confidence.

3. **Team Leader:** Usually the founder. The face of the brand. This person may not be involved in communications regularly, but showing your community who the leader is behind the brand displays credibility and transparency. Bring them in for special events or communications, such as a Q&A video or an intro post.

4. **Beta User(s):** This includes anyone who may have access to beta units. These individuals should engage on social media, post photos, videos, and answer questions on their use of the product as the first adopters. This boosts social proof, credibility, and gives prospective customers access to someone who knows the product but is not necessarily part of the core team.

Launch Marketers Have Six Senses

You have one shot at launch day. All your hard work, investment, and preparation come together like the pieces of a puzzle. And, like a puzzle, just one missing piece can ruin it.

Once, after spending three hours cooking a grand dinner of roast chicken for my family, I realized as I started to serve the veggies that I'd forgotten to turn the oven on, and the chicken remained uncooked! One missing piece had ruined the entire dinner, just as one missing piece can ruin a launch. It's never obvious what that missing piece is— it's not fluorescent pink or extra large. It's often hidden, and while it might seem small, it can make or break your success. Unfortunately, just like me and my cooking mishap, many entrepreneurs don't realize they're missing a puzzle piece until it's too late. At that point, they can't recoup their time or backtrack in the launch process. They've missed their chance to complete their puzzle and deliver a successful launch.

It's human nature to have a hard time identifying problems you can't see. In his book *The Personal MBA*, Josh Kaufman calls this "absence blindness." As he explains, what makes a manager effective in a leadership role is their ability to overcome absence blindness by anticipating likely issues and resolving them before they become larger problems. The same is true when you're launching a business. The need to overcome absence blindness is especially important. There are rarely second chances or opportunities to rewind. As an entrepreneur, you must anticipate the often-invisible barriers your target audience might experience that prevent them from buying and resolve those barriers in advance (yet another example of how risk aversion is an asset when launching a business).

I agree with Kaufman, too, that there's only one thing that can help avoid absence blindness: experience. Experience provides the expert a bigger mental database of information, and more data means more of an ability to spot patterns in that data. Experience in launch marketing allows the expert to find patterns in data that suggest an absence (a missing puzzle piece). They can "see" that something isn't quite right and work to resolve the problem before it's too late (search for the missing puzzle piece, find a replacement, or start again with a fresh puzzle).

Fortunately, you don't have to acquire this experience yourself. You bought this book and can tap into my mental database. My sixth sense is now yours, too. Together, we can go through the most common sales objections you will experience during a launch. Sprinkle these solutions into your pre-launch strategy as part of your communication with prospective customers, proactively solving the objections before it's too late.

Common Sales Objections & How to Solve Them

There are six broad categories that we can fit most sales objections into:

1. Cost
2. Product
3. Brand
4. Technical
5. Apathy
6. Timing

Let's explore common sales objections within each of these and how you can solve them.

1. Cost

Objection: It's too expensive.
Solution: Roughly one-third of prospects that choose not to take you up on your offer do so because they feel it's too expensive.[1] This number has been consistent during the past decade. There are limited opportunities to solve this. However, launch campaigns allow you to offer deals

that you won't be able to offer longer term. Emphasize this. Never again will potential buyers be able to purchase your offer at a price this low—this is their one chance. If your offer went through the validation step of this system and passed, then you can solve price objections. If you skipped validation and are only now getting negative feedback on the price point, you may have to rewind and start again.

Objection: It's too expensive for me to buy right now.
Solution: A couple of neat options here. If you can identify the prospects this objection pertains to, offer a delayed deadline for them to take advantage of the launch deal. Give them an extra 30 days or perhaps 90 days and make sure they know you're bending your rules just for them. Make them feel special. Alternatively, multiple payments are another good resolution to try, particularly for higher priced products. Give folks the option to pay in installments, putting a deposit down now and making another payment or so at intervals. This makes it more manageable for them and captures a sale you might not have otherwise received.

Objection: I already bought this from another company.
Solution: If they love what they've got from your competitor, there's not much you can do. You might consider giving them a special guarantee (money back) or look to focus on your unique selling propositions and use cases versus the competition.

Objection: Shipping costs too much money.
Solution: Shipping cost is the no. 1 reason for e-commerce cart abandonment, according to data collected by Statistica.[2] People hate paying for shipping. A good tip for any launch campaign is to offer free shipping and increase the cost of the product offer itself in order to balance out your shipping costs. You'll see a better conversion rate selling a product for $75 and free shipping, than selling for $50 and charging $25 to ship.

Objection: Shipping costs too much time.

<u>Solution</u>: Time is money, and this is very apparent when it comes to shipping timelines. This is one you'll look to solve well before it rears its head. If you're expecting a longer shipping timeline (a main sales objection faced by folks who use crowdfunding platforms, such as Indiegogo or Kickstarter), be clear about this upfront. There's no point wasting marketing dollars on potential customers who love your idea but want it now if they're not going to get it for six months. Only focus your acquisition on prospects who would be willing to wait.

2. Product

Objection: I don't understand how it's different from/better than other, similar products.

<u>Solution</u>: Back in Chapter 3, you identified the unique things about your offer to which people are attracted. If potential buyers give you an objection about the product, it means you haven't made these unique traits clear enough in your marketing. Comparison charts, videos, and graphics that zero-in on what makes your offer stand out over the competition is the way to resolve this. Leave your prospects without a question in their mind as to what it is that makes your offer different (and better). The sooner you can introduce this difference into your marketing, the less you'll face this objection.

Objection: I don't trust the product does what you say it does.

<u>Solution</u>: This is a hurdle that new, innovative products tend to face frequently. People don't need help understanding how a pair of socks work. They might, however, question how a product that allows you to breathe underwater works. If your idea is something never seen before, recognize that the onus is on you to explain the technology/design behind it and instill the credibility that it works as you say it does. How-to videos, product guides, specs sheets, behind-the-scenes peeks at your process, and third-party credibility, such as reviews, are all solutions to use.

3. **Brand**

Objection: I don't know if I can trust you.
Solution: You'll get this a lot, particularly on your first product launch. In this case, you have three major facets of your product or service to emphasize:

- Transparency (into your founders, company, production process, design)
- Credibility (your experience, past success, top notch customer service, prototype testing, partners)
- Minimizing the risk for the user (warranties, money-back guarantees, other customer reviews, product certifications, brand awards)

The more you can be upfront and honest with prospective customers, the higher your chance of building trust.

Objection: I don't trust your website with my payment information.
Solution: If you're a new company with a new website and a never-before-heard-of offer, people are well within their right mind to be cautious about handing over personal information. Trust badges are a way to go here. Actual Insights found that 75 percent of people feel trust badges increase the perceived trustworthiness of a brand.[3] Additionally, SSL website security protocols, and using trusted payment processors, such as Paypal or Apple Pay, can be critical to making someone feel safe enough to give you their credit card information.

4. **Technical**

Objection: Your website timed me out/has browser issues/is buggy.
Solution: A technical issue like this should never become an objection in the first place. In this case, a potential customer wants to buy your product but can't. In all the years of marketing product launches, I

have yet to work on a launch that doesn't experience this objection for at least a few of their launch customers. It can be caused by the most minor technical error, and where and how it places itself in your launch can be almost impossible to predict. Yet many entrepreneurs overlook it. Do your best to preemptively spot this type of issue well before you start marketing your idea to prospective customers by running through all your flows as if you were a prospective customer. Check landing page sign-ups, receive your own promotional emails, act as a buyer on prospect calls, buy your own product on your site. Do these things on a mobile device, a tablet, and a desktop. Do them in different browsers and on different operating systems. Find the bugs before your customers do.

Objection: I expressed interest but never heard from you again.
Solution: The first place to look in many situations like this is user error. The number of people that add their email addresses or phone numbers incorrectly to sign up forms or checkout flows is surprisingly high. If you're being reactive, check your prospect information manually and review what users have input. If you're being proactive, there are tools and apps you can use to avoid obviously incorrect information (such as email addresses that are "gnail.com" rather than "gmail.com") being submitted by the user.

Objection: My payment was declined.
Solution: Address this personally. Perhaps it's a blip with the payment processor or perhaps an issue with their payment method. Either way, if a prospective customer has got this far, they're worth pursuing after falling at the final hurdle. Email them or call them and offer alternative payment options.

5. **Apathy**

Objection: I don't see why I need to do this now rather than another time in the future.
<u>Solution</u>: Many good ways to solve this one, such as setting deadlines to offers and deals ("24 hours only"), adding bonus incentives for fast action ("buy today and get a free accessory"), highlighting price increases ("prices jump tomorrow") or countdown timers ("only 23 hours left"), and emphasizing scarcity ("only 3 available at this price").

Objection: I'm just window shopping.
<u>Solution</u>: These are the folks you don't want in your funnel in the first place at launch and take us back to our discussions around purchase intent in Chapter 2. The sooner you can work out which type of prospective customers have intent to buy and which are just browsing, the sooner you can focus your efforts on those who are priority. The moment you start acquiring prospective buyers, make sure there are insights being collected that help you distinguish between real buyers and window shoppers.

Objection: I was interested but I'm not anymore.
<u>Solution</u>: If they've lost interest, you may be out of options. You might want to try a Hail Mary, such as a big, one-time discount or a really personal approach (like requesting a one-on-one phone call). More likely, this is a group you may want to simply move on from. Your energy could be better placed elsewhere.

6. **Timing**
Timing is a particularly challenging objection, as it's not necessarily an objection of which the consumer is aware. Unlike the others mentioned above, you can't lay out the objection and a specific solution. This particular hurdle is too unique. However, it certainly deserves a mention in this chapter.

According to Bill Gross, founder of more than 100 companies, the most important factor in achieving success versus failure was timing. In fact, he suggested it could account for a whopping 42 percent of the difference between success and failure. Similar to how the entrepreneurship world incorrectly glamorizes risk, it also often incorrectly praises being first to market. Although "first movers" face some advantages in particular industries, the research generally does not support an overall first-mover advantage. After all, consider that "first movers" are the ones that make the mistakes, while those coming in behind them can learn from those very mistakes without the repercussions of suffering them. Additionally, since the market gets more defined as more companies enter it with new iterations on solutions, the focus is on providing superior quality rather than determining what exactly the solution should be.

This all goes to say that there may be a situation you face in which you've checked many of the right boxes in developing your idea and preparing for a launch, but the timing is simply not right to deliver success. The world may just not be ready for your solution. While this is a problem somewhat outside of your control, it's an objection you should uncover well before the product becomes available to the public. This is precisely the type of red flag that validation would discover and put a stop to you moving forward. If you skipped validation and this timing issue is news to you, you may have to go back and start over.

Discovering Objections Unique to Your Launch

While the previous section will cover 90 percent of the objections you face at launch, I can't predict your future. There will also be sales objections unique to your launch that you'll need to identify and resolve. Two common ways to do this are through qualitative data collection (such as surveys) and quantitative data collection (such as web analytics).

Collecting prospect feedback

Finding out why people won't buy doesn't have to wait until you're live and selling. By asking the right questions before your launch, you'll be able to make an accurate and data-driven guess at what the unique objections to your offer will be in the future. After someone has expressed interest in your offer, have them answer a few questions. You could include a simple survey on the post-sign-up thank-you page or in a welcome email, or you could ask directly in an offline marketing scenario.

Here's one particularly useful question we always include in pre-launch surveys in our system: "Is there anything else you'd like to know about [PRODUCT OFFER] or do you have any feedback for us before we launch?"

Leave that question open-ended and you'll get all sorts of replies that show you what your current marketing content is missing in order to achieve the sale. Get questions on warranties? Add or highlight these more clearly. Hear negative feedback on a particular feature? Address it. See the same requests over and over, such as for how-to videos, user guides, or specs sheets? Publish them as soon as possible. Common questions in surveys like this can also be the foundation of your product or company FAQ.

For an extra level of engagement, make sure you collect contact information from those who ask questions and expect a response. For example, you can add a second, simple question: "Would you like a personal response to your question from the [PRODUCT OFFER] team? If so, please enter your email address below." Adding a question in what appears to be a generic survey and receiving a personal response from the founder is a pleasant surprise for many consumers and a powerful relationship-builder between the brand and the end user.

Analyzing your data

As Steve Jobs once said, "It's really hard to design products by focus groups. A lot of times, people don't know what they want until you show it to them." User surveys are not the whole picture; you should be looking at user behavior when viewing your offer, too.

Using analytics tools such as Google Analytics and Hotjar Analytics, and testing platforms like Unbounce, KickOff Labs, or Nostra, will enable you to uncover trends or objections that don't appear otherwise. Perhaps you note that people are clicking on one particular area of your site or feature of your product more than any other, which tells you that you'll need more content and more answers for that area or feature (if it's the most interesting part of your offer, it can also lead to the biggest objections).

Or perhaps you're running a validation and notice that people are very keen to express interest in your offer, but the numbers drop off a cliff when they see the price and are asked to put down a small reservation payment. This tells you that you've hit the right note in drawing interest, but still have some work to do on your pricing and positioning before moving forward into a full launch.

Honesty Is the Best Policy

A few years ago, a friend of mine was moving into a new apartment. We were hanging out one afternoon as he prepared for the move, and he was showing me the dining room furniture he planned to order online for his new place. We were scrolling through the pictures on his phone, and it looked like real top-notch stuff; the photos were fantastic. And, he'd apparently managed to find a brilliant deal, as he was going to be getting the dining room table and chairs for less than half the price I had paid for mine just a few months before.

A couple of weeks later, I received several text messages from my friend in quick succession, each a photo. The dining room furniture had arrived. And it was nothing like he had expected.

Firstly, it was toddler-size. Yes, that's right, he'd somehow ordered what was essentially a play set for children. Secondly, it was made of shoddy brown plastic that broke into pieces with relatively little pressure. Nothing like the strong and sturdy, classic oak wood that it appeared to be in the photos online.

What a disaster! We can have a laugh about it now and we often do, reminiscing about the six-week period when he was literally having breakfast, lunch, and dinner at the kids table while he waited for adult furniture to arrive. Yet it's an example of what consumers deal with on a regular basis—buying a product and the reality being nothing like their expectation. From the era of the Nigerian Prince email scam in the 1990s to the more advanced schemes you see today, the internet has created a world where the consumer has less and less trust in the seller. To take a quote from my favorite movie, *Forrest Gump*, "You never know what you're gonna get" when buying something from a new brand or someone you don't know.

This unfortunate reality is why trust is so, so critical when launching a new idea to an audience who doesn't know you. As highlighted earlier in this chapter, credibility is key. In addition to some of the marketing tactics mentioned previously, such as warranties, payment security, and money-back guarantees, there are a couple of quite simple things that you, as the creator, can do to build credibility and trust with your community of prospective customers.

Be Transparent

According to a study by Label Insight, 94 percent of buyers are more likely to be loyal to brands that are transparent and 56 percent would stay loyal to a brand for life if it was completely open and transparent.[4] It's not hard to understand the data: when you think of an entrepreneur or company who you feel is honest with you as opposed to one who hides something, which one are you more likely to buy from and support?

I see this in launches all the time. During launch campaigns for new products, there will always be some level of cancelation from the buyers. People change their mind or have unexpected expenses arise that they need to prioritize. For creators and entrepreneurs who are honest, transparent, and open with their audience (about things like their team, manufacturing, timelines, product specifications, etc.), the cancelation rate/refund rate from their launch customers might be 4 percent to 6 percent. For creators and entrepreneurs who are more opaque (not having their company information easy to find online, not communicating with the community often enough, not answering questions that arise in a speedy fashion), the cancelation rate/refund rate will likely be closer to 15 percent to 20 percent.

With the size of launches that our clients usually target, the difference between a 5 percent cancelation rate and 15 percent rate can be hundreds of thousands of dollars. It's a tremendous amount of money that can make or break a business. Yet it's so solvable, given it's almost solely down to the fact that consumers are wary of being duped. If they don't know you and you're not open and honest with them, why should they trust you?

Be Accessible

One of the most famous customer service stories is about the glasses brand we touched on earlier in this book, Warby Parker. In the story, a customer, in his hurry to disembark a train at his station, left a pair of glasses onboard. He was in luck, however. A short while later, he received both his original glasses and a replacement pair in the mail, thanks to his seatmate on the train, former Warby Parker General Counsel Anjail Kumar.

Such customer experiences are impossible to replicate at scale, every day. Yet anyone launching a new product or idea should be looking for as many of these opportunities to "wow" as possible. You might not see a Facebook post go viral about your generosity the first time you do something like this, or the second, or ever. But such acts build up the positive image of you and your new brand. Day by day, act by act, this goodwill builds. With time, word of mouth between customers leads to you becoming known as the entrepreneur and brand with unbelievable customer service.

This shows a high-level of accessibility from a brand. In launch marketing, accessibility is a measure of how *accessible* the brand team members are to the public. Are they hidden behind an anonymous Contact Us form, or are members of the executive team/the founders willingly and regularly speaking directly with their potential customers? The more accessible you can be, the more trust you can build. After all, who doesn't feel special when the CEO of a brand personally reaches out? Or when the company founder is the one responding to their question?

When working with the bedding brand Sheets & Giggles on the launch of the company and their first-ever eucalyptus bed sheets, it would be common to see the Sheets & Giggles founder having full-on, hours-long conversations with the prospective buyers. Facebook Messenger conversations or email threads covering a wide array of topics, such as their families and friends, local food specialties, the best vacation spots, or friendly banter about recent sports events. He showed authentic, genuine interest in, and respect for, his potential customers. In return, they paid such accessibility back many times over when it came to the launch of the brand, both in terms of buying the product and spreading the word with friends and family.

What's more, while it's not possible to give every customer or community member an experience like this, lessons can be drawn from brands with leading customer experience tactics.

At the time of writing this, on arriving at Warby Parker's website, visitors can take a quiz. This is a fun and engaging introduction to the brand.

When they launched, Sheets & Giggles had "easter eggs" sprinkled throughout their launch marketing strategies. (Easter eggs are hidden messages or rewards inserted in marketing emails, in ads, and on web pages, like a treasure hunt.) The eggs are often well hidden, so that users find it gratifying when they discover them and excited when rewarded, helping form bonds between the creator (brand) and finders (customers). The image below shows an example of a Sheets & Giggles easter egg on their Indiegogo launch page. It's hidden due to the small font and location directly below an image, which draws your attention.

We also use a closed loop manufacturing process (so the byproducts are reused in the process itself), which results in a near zero environmental impact.

Timeline

Oct. '17 - April '18	May 2018	August 2018	Q4 2018
R&D, Design, Testing	Indiegogo Preorder	Shipping Preorders	You Are Now Asleep

Take a screenshot of this and email it to easteregg@sheetsgiggles.com with your order number, and we'll upgrade your order with a free gift. (Don't tell anyone.) Easter Egg 2 of 4.

These are just a couple of examples of providing a fun brand experience that can be scaled across all customers. In today's customer-centric world, the power has shifted so buyers now have the upper hand. They can easily choose who they do and don't want to engage with. Building trust is even more integral at the start of the launch journey.

As a launch marketer and creator, your job is not just to obtain and convert potential customers, but to delight and retain these people. The best way to do this? Transparency, accessibility, and great customer service.

No One Is an Island

In his book *Atomic Habits*, the author James Clear speaks to how we tend to imitate others in our habits. In particular, we prioritize three social groups: the close (family and friends), the many (the tribe), and the powerful (those with status and prestige).

Purchasing habits and conformity habits sit slap bang in the middle of a launch marketing strategy. Being part of a community and conforming to behaviors approved by that community are integral in order to thrive. No one is an island. To put it into terms we discussed earlier in the book, no one likes to eat at an empty restaurant.

It's the job of the launch strategy to prioritize the three social groups highlighted by Clear and engineer imitation in each of them. Consider the now-famous experiment by Solomon Asch (also highlighted by Clear in his book) on social conformity. In the study, 50 students from Swarthmore College, in Pennsylvania, participated in a "vision test." Using a line judgment task (lines drawn next to each other and participants are instructed to state which comparison line was most similar in length to the primary, target line), Asch put a naive participant in a room with seven actors.

The actors had agreed in advance what their responses would be, however ridiculous that answer might seem to an outsider. After all, the lines were drawn in a manner whereby it was clearly obvious which comparison line was closest in length to the primary, target line. The real participant did not know this and was led to believe that the other seven actors were also real participants.

Each person in the room had to state aloud which comparison line (A, B, or C) was most like the target line. The real participant sat at the end of the row and gave his or her answer last.

Over the 12 critical trials, about 75 percent of participants conformed at least once. In the control group, with no pressure to conform to confederates, less than 1 percent of participants gave the wrong answer. That's a huge difference. Again, the answer was always obvious.

The real participant knew when they were giving a wrong answer that they were doing so, yet still conformed to the group. Clearly, people are susceptible to following the crowd, even if they don't necessarily agree with the crowd's decision.

Let's consider how to engineer imitation in each of these groups within the Five-Step High-Profit Launch System:

The close (family and friends)

Picture this: you're in need of a plumber and have two options. The first is a lifelong friend of your cousin. They are affordable and highly recommended by your cousin and his wife. The second is from an ad you saw on the highway, a chap claiming to be the "no. 1 in town at rock-bottom prices."

Who do you choose? Most would go with the first choice, the lifelong friend of your close family member. According to a study by Nielson, 92 percent of consumers believe recommendations from their friends and family over all forms of advertising.[5] While sharing information via word-of-mouth recommendations is the oldest form of marketing, what's changed is how social media and the digital world allows this to happen at scale and quickly within extended social circles. In an instant, one person's recommendation of a brand through their Instagram or Twitter profile can reach thousands (if not millions) of people, whether it be friends, family, or followers.

Reviews, recommendations, and referrals have a greater impact coming from someone like us, someone in our social circle, who we know and trust. This is why anyone launching an idea should focus on incentivizing the earliest supporters to help spread the word among their social circles.

One of the more famous word-of-mouth initiatives in launch marketing was that of Harry's, the New York–based grooming brand. They focused on building a referral campaign that helped people to spread the word to their friends.

The campaign was relatively simple—a two-step funnel. First, prospective buyers entered their email addresses on a landing page registering their interest in the product. Following the signup, the prospects were taken to a web page that contained a shareable link to the first landing page, coded specifically to each individual who signed up. Below the link were buttons for the prospect to share the link through email, Facebook, and Twitter with the click of a mouse. By sharing the link with friends, users had the opportunity to earn free products. The more friends who signed up using the unique referral link, the bigger the prize. In short, users would be rewarded by sharing the product with their friends.

A simple referral funnel like this helped Harry's acquire 100,000 prospective buyers into their community before they launched, achieved due to the magic of word-of-mouth marketing and the speed at which communication can occur via the internet.

The many (the tribe)

The Dutch tulip bulb market bubble, also known as Tulipmania, was one of the most famous market bubbles and crashes of all time. It occurred in Holland during the 1600s when huge demand drove the value of tulip bulbs to extremes. At the height of the market, the rarest tulip bulbs traded for as much as six times the average person's annual salary.

Tulipmania isn't dissimilar from the effect a crowd—and demand—can have on the perceived value of a product or idea at launch. If more people appear to want it, then the value perception and the desire for others to obtain it increases.

Another, more contemporary, way to look at how "the many" can impact an individual's behavior is FOMO, or fear of missing out: the uneasy feeling that you're missing out, exacerbated by the photoshopped and faked world of social media. We see thousands of other people participating in the latest trend and we want in.

When launching a product, this effect can be engineered in a few ways:

- **Make your crowd visible.** One of the components of crowd-funding websites, like Indiegogo, that makes them successful is that the number of backers and funding total are front and center of the campaign. The moment a new potential customer sees the web page of a successful launch, they are able to see just how many people have jumped onboard. If they see that 5,000 others have supported this launch with their hard-earned cash, then they are more likely to do so, too.
- **Create scarcity.** If you have ever tried getting tickets to a concert of a world-famous musician or a table at a Michelin star restaurant, you know that such things can feel near impossible. Why? Because there's limited availability—scarcity. There's much, much more demand than supply. Creating limited availability for an offer means prospective buyers have no choice but to act fast, leading to a high level of traction quickly and creating a powerful snowball effect.
- **Incentivize positive urgency.** A close cousin of scarcity (which could be perceived as a stick rather than a carrot—those who don't act fast are punished), positive urgency is more of a carrot—rewarding those who act quickly. You see this often on TV infomercials, where the charming gentleman and beautiful women on screen are urging viewers to call in quickly and make their purchase, as the first 100 customers get a freebie accessory included in their order.

The powerful (those with status and prestige)

If you ever see a photo of me in my later teen years, you may very well see me sporting a dashing faux-hawk hairstyle with blond highlights. The reason was David Beckham. I don't tend to follow many celebrity trends these days, but the younger me was much more malleable. Those with status and prestige are instrumental in forming our behaviors. While we might think we're free, independent thinkers, we're suckers for following in the steps of others we admire and their attributes. In my case as a teenager, this was Beckham and his hair.

In fact, according to research by Harvard Business School professor Anita Elberse and Barclays Capital analyst Jeroen Verleun, a celebrity endorsement increases a company's sales an average of 4 percent relative to its competition and also increases a company's stock value by 0.25 percent.[6] Clearly, when trying to corral people around a product or idea, the impact of endorsements from those with status and prestige can be monumental.

Powerful doesn't have to mean famous, rich, or well known. Sure, a shoutout from a famous celebrity is a great example of a nice endorsement and boost of credibility, but it can go well beyond that. After all, not everyone has the funds to bring a Kardashian onboard.

If you're launching a health product, doctors could be considered powerful endorsements. If you're pitching an idea for how to get a great night's sleep, those who suffer from insomnia may offer the most prestige in persuading others. Or, if you're fundraising for a charitable cause, those benefiting from the cause could offer the most useful credibility.

Each of these examples speaks to how you can use assets available to almost everyone—such as family, friends—and psychological tactics—like urgency and FOMO—to engineer imitation among a group of prospective buyers. This is a form of marketing engagement, which serves as the fuel to your launch fire. Use these engagement methods to pull the right triggers, and the growth at launch can quickly become exponential.

What Does Engagement Actually Look Like?

You might be thinking that it's one thing reading through all these ideas, and something entirely different to put it into practice. With that in mind, I wanted to shed light on the type of engagement communications my team and I might share with a community of prospective customers as we prepare a product for launch. Seeing what we do may help you to bridge the gap from theory to practice. Consider these as marketing emails, group messages, videos, or even social media posts. What's more important here is the message being conveyed, not the platform on which you present it.

Brand Story: A communication that introduces potential customers to the brand, the founders, and their journey to-date in bringing this idea to life. This is an opportunity to build trust between founders and their communities.

Additional Touchpoint Invite: A communication that incentivizes potential customers to connect with you in an additional way (for example, ask folks on an email list to join an SMS list, too). This is an opportunity to maximize your chance to reach your community with your product offer on the day you launch.

Launch Timeline Reminder: A communication that reminds your community about important milestones, such as your launch date or your shipping date. This is an opportunity to ensure customers are aware of dates that are key to your success.

Customer FAQ: A communication that shares a handful of the most commonly asked questions from your potential customers. This is an opportunity to make information more public and visible to your community, reducing questions down the line and potentially resolving some of your sales objections.

Founder Q&A: A communication that allows your community to ask the founder(s) questions. This is an opportunity to create transparency, build trust, and potentially resolve some of your sales objections.

Social Proof: A communication that initiates FOMO among your community, by sharing testimonials from beta users, positive comments on your ads or from your surveys, or any data that highlights the excitement folks have for your offer. This is an opportunity to increase anticipation and drive urgency.

Use-Cases: A communication (or multiple communications) that showcases core use-cases for your product. This is an opportunity to help potential customers visualize how they could use your product.

Benefits: A communication (or multiple communications) that showcases core benefits or the USPs of your product. This is an opportunity to help potential customers better understand how they could benefit from your product.

Objection Resolutions: A communication (or multiple communications) that directly responds to any specific sales objections you're seeing among your community. This is an opportunity to resolve objections among many community members, without having to respond to or communicate with folks individually.

Credibility: A communication that shares the credibility you have and why your community can have confidence in their buying decision. Examples could be media visibility, well-known folks on your team or advisory board, collaborations or partnerships with famous brands or people, and certifications or studies that prove the efficacy of your product. This is an opportunity to increase trust between the brand and your potential customers.

Grandy Gets Ready to Launch

Let's check back in with Grandy's Glorious Bakery and see how the GGB team handled the Audience Engagement step.

1. After three weeks of building our Pre-Launch Sign-Up List of people interested in Grandy's bakery, we sent two emails to this group. One was an introduction to Grandy (a personal video of her saying hello from the kitchen, apron on and ingredients spread across the countertop). The second, a week later, was an announcement of a launch day gathering. This would be a bake sale in Grandy's front yard, where Grandy's goods would be on sale for the first time ever, and those who had signed up could come and take advantage of their discount. While the business itself would exist online, this real-world event at launch was an opportunity to build awareness and excitement around Grandy's goodies.

    For our communication strategy, we knew that food (and baking, in particular) is often more than just a biological need. People have an emotional relationship with it. As a result, trust-related sales objections are much more common among culinary businesses. The transparency, openness, and personalization of a video from Grandy herself went a long way toward building a bond between Grandy and her audience. She reminded them of their grandparents and the fond memories they had of family baking. This approach resolved any trust-related sales objections and made sure there were no objections in understanding how/where to take advantage of the offer.

2. To really spice things up, we also said that we would extend the launch discount of the first 20 customers for an entire year. We knew that if we got a small crowd to our website and front yard bake sale early, the ripple effect would kick in. With this

new offer, people had a real, strong incentive to arrive as soon as possible and be one of the first in line. This helped solve the objection of a lack of credibility (no one wants to eat in an empty restaurant).

3. We made sure that the baked goods looked incredibly attractive in our photos and video, but we knew that it was the taste that would make or break this launch day bonanza. We also knew that these treats were addictive. If you had a bite, you'd want a batch. With that in mind, we made sure everyone in our audience knew that there would be free samples at our launch day event. We were extremely confident that: (a) free samples would drive attendance (who doesn't want free cake?) and (b) once someone had eaten a sample, they'd have their money out to buy right away. This tactic helped resolve objections about the quality of the product and the risk of customers feeling like they'd wasted their money. If they tried the product first, they knew for sure that they would be getting treats of excellent quality once they purchased them.

4. We also looked ahead to potential sales objections during the launch itself, planning the event so the garden would be accessible and friendly, and streamlining the website so it would be concise, clean, and ready to accept orders. We prepared a layout for the baked goods that day, with clear signage as to what treats were available and at which table. We knew that if we laid out dozens of delicacies on one table, only four or five people would be able to see what was on offer at any one time, prohibiting sales, so we spread them out across the garden. The house is on a quiet road, so we also planned to make sure there was plenty of signage on two nearby busier streets so that people would know where to go. Finally, we tested the website and its checkout functionality across different computers, mobile devices, and payment methods to ensure anyone visiting the website would be able to easily make their order once we launched.

5. In the week prior to the launch, we instructed close friends and family to arrive 15 minutes early to the launch day event. This ensured any non-familial customers would see at least a dozen people at the launch event, socializing and indulging in the baked treats, by the time they arrived. A bustling garden was vital to drawing attention from neighbors and those living on nearby streets.

Grandy had worked hard and felt confident, but the butterflies in her stomach had already begun. She knew that, despite the great results so far, she couldn't take anything for granted. You never quite know what the customer reaction will be once your business launches, and, with launch day fast approaching, the feeling of uncertainty was growing stronger.

My Favorite Tools

During the Audience Engagement step, you'll find me using:

- **Unbounce:** Landing page builder for us to design, develop, test, and optimize launch marketing web pages.
- **Stripe:** Payment processor to collect 1 percent reservations.
- **Klaviyo:** Email marketing and SMS marketing platform, where we can collect and communicate with our email and SMS communities.
- **Google Forms:** Simple survey tool to collect answers from prospective customers.
- **Facebook Groups:** Spaces on the Facebook platform that deliver an open and transparent line of communication between founders and potential customers.
- **Google Analytics:** Analytics platform that allows us to evaluate the behavior and performance of our web traffic.
- **Databox:** Analytics dashboard that allows us to collate marketing from different platforms in one, clean view.
- **Adobe Creative Suite:** Software we use for graphic design, video editing, web development, and photography.
- **Google Drive:** My go-to file storage platform where we keep any and every document, PowerPoint, graphic, analysis, and folder created during a launch.
- **KickOff Labs:** Sweepstakes platform that allows us to create and track viral referral programs.

CHAPTER SIX

Keep Your Launch Simple

N THIS CHAPTER, you'll learn about Audience Conversion, Step 4 of the Five-Step High-Profit Launch System, including:

- How to ensure your launch offer is primed to turn prospects into customers
- The two types of launch trajectories, *the tortoise* and *the hare*, and which is right for you
- Why your pumped-up pre-launch community may have a change of heart and reject the offer they've been excited about (and what you can do to get them back)

This should be done following completion of the previous chapters (Audience Acquisition and Audience Engagement), *only* once your pre-launch community is acquired, engaged, and ready to buy. It is recommended you allow yourself one to three months to complete the strategies in this chapter, depending on the launch trajectory you choose to pursue.

You Have Seven Seconds—Make Them Count

At this stage, you've spent weeks, months, or maybe even years going through the first three steps. You've validated your idea, acquired an audience of excited, potential customers, and worked hard to resolve any barriers to the sale that may have existed among them.

Now, it's time to launch.

At this point, it is critical that you keep your message simple. Our attention span has decreased dramatically in the past two decades, from roughly 12 seconds at the turn of the millennium to just seven or eight seconds today.[1] That's probably less time than it took you to read that sentence. As we can see in web analytics, users often leave web pages within seconds of arriving. A recent study suggests that slow-loading websites cost retailers $2.6 billion in lost sales each year.[2] It's madness, but it's the hand we're dealt as online entrepreneurs. You have seven seconds—make them count.

This means you must prioritize and simplify your efforts. In the world of crowdfunding (one of the most popular launch avenues for new products), a launch video has traditionally been key. One of the biggest mistakes crowdfunding campaigners make is investing too much time and money on an elaborate launch video. Does it look great? Sure. But most people only care about two things when it comes to a launch video: what it is offering and how it will benefit them. The special effects, the hours some folks spend trying to get the humor, or worse, lengthy narratives, just right, often do very little to entice someone to buy.

Another way early entrepreneurs often overdo things is writing verbose copy. A mentor of mine once looked at a wordy draft of a marketing email I had written. With one glance, she said: "Cut every third word," and handed it back to me. That's stuck with me ever since. It's not a universal rule, but a nice reminder to keep things as short as possible. A good rule of thumb is KISS (keep it simple, stupid). Keeping things simple, concise, and direct allows you to make those seven seconds count.

I like to focus on KISS in all of my communications, from marketing to managing, personal to professional. In fact, my family often remarks on my one-word or one-line email and text responses. KISS is part and parcel of everything I do. It traces its roots back to my dad, and his love of conversation.

My dad loves to talk. When I was a young kid, he would embarrass me by talking to anyone and everyone, in shops, on the street, or at school. Now, as an adult, I appreciate his chattiness as an invaluable personality trait, but I felt differently growing up. His love for the sound of his own voice led him to become an avid member of Toastmasters International (a nonprofit organization offering opportunities for members to hone their public speaking and presentation skills), where he's still toasting to this day. When I was old enough, my dad convinced me to join him as a member. During my speech preparations for the group, he would always remind me: "Will, keep it simple. Just tell them what you're going to tell them, then tell them, and then tell them what you told them."

After more than 10 years of experience in marketing, I would recommend adding a fourth line to this principle: tell them what to do next (known in marketing as a call to action).

1. Tell them what you're going to tell them.
2. Tell them.
3. Tell them what you told them.
4. Tell what to do next.

Could it be any simpler than that?

When you launch, one of the most important places to apply the KISS principle is your landing page. A landing page is where most people interested in your offer will end up making a purchase, so it's important that it's easy for them to understand and use. While what you're selling may change, the purpose of your landing page should remain constant: to capture the interest, attention, and purchasing power of your prospects in less time than it took you to read this sentence.

Another important place to apply the KISS principle in your launch is how you treat and interact with your customers (known as customer experience or customer service). Customer service is a critical part of a successful business launch. After weeks or months of anticipation, people can finally buy what you're selling—and they'll have questions. When my company launches a new product with a client, we set up a timetable that ensures potential customers have 24-hour access to customer service for the first two days. Whether it be via a phone number, an email address, or an instant chat tool, give your prospective customers instant access to someone on your launch team to answer all of their questions.

Add a sprinkling of personalization (make each prospect feel special), urgency (why they should act now), and social validation (seeing others take action), and you've got yourself a recipe for converting potential customers into buyers.

Make it personal

Everyone wants to be made to feel special, and the recipients of launch marketing are no different. While many decry the invasiveness of advertising, recent studies suggest a third of customers wish their shopping experience was more personalized.[3]

Absolute transparency and open communication with potential customers are effective ways to personalize the relationship. Another is to create segments of audiences, to ensure folks only receive the information most relevant to them (for example, ensuring buyers in California and not offering ads for a product only available in the UK).

Curating the offer as something just for them through your marketing adds a level of trust and intimacy that makes your offer more appealing to its recipient.

Make it urgent

We've discussed urgency previously in the book. Nowhere is it more important than when looking to convert your audience at launch. Limiting the number of units, products, tickets, seats, or services (whatever it is you're selling) at different pricing tiers is one fundamental way to get folks acting fast. They want to grab the offer at the lowest price possible, before one tier runs out and another pricing tier begins.

Additionally, I like to make what I call a "scarecrow" offer highly visible. This is a decoy offer or pricing tier, showing a big jump in cost for the buyer if they don't take action right away. For example, you might offer a launch price of $99 with a scarecrow offer alongside it of $199. This "scares" the buyer away from the high price and pushes them to take early action. This might be a price jump of 50 percent or 100 percent, more than perhaps a 10 percent to 20 percent increase a buyer might see in the earlier pricing tier options. This is more emphatic.

You can also consider launch day bonuses for the first customers, such as free add-ons or accessories you can bundle in with the main product purchase. To drive urgency, these should only be available for the first customers (perhaps the first 50 or all day-one buyers).

Make it unmissable

We also touched on FOMO previously: the fear of missing out. By making the eager crowd visible and highlighting the appearance of high demand for the offer, those on the sidelines will want to jump in before it's too late.

Such influence can come from tactics such as

- Peer pressure (being enticed to perform a behavior by seeing those in the same social group as you performing that behavior, such as seeing your friends sharing the same experience on Instagram)
- Social validation (performing a behavior due to the approval you will get from others for it, such as working hard in your job to earn a promotion)
- Influencer credibility (performing a behavior because someone you admire does it, such as buying new trainers due to your favorite sportsperson advertising them)

The way to get people to act fast is to make them fear the alternative—missing out by not acting fast enough.

Are You the Tortoise or the Hare?

In *Aesop's Fables, The Tortoise and the Hare* is the account of a race between a tortoise (a slow and steady mover) and a hare (an animal with explosive speed). You've likely heard the story. The hare's speed makes him arrogant. Confident of victory, the hare takes a nap midway through the race. When the hare awakens, he finds that the tortoise, crawling slowly but steadily, has arrived before him.

I like to reference this fable in launch marketing, not because slow and steady is the better option but because it's a wonderful analogy of the two types of trajectories entrepreneurs and creators can pursue in their launches. Let's take a look at each:

The Tortoise

The Tortoise launch trajectory is slow, steady, and focused on incremental improvements over a longer period of time. An entrepreneur going this route will often launch without much fanfare. Instead, they opt to stay under the radar and make improvements to their launch marketing day by day. They tend to consider reaching their destination (a goal, such as revenue or customers) as a marathon, rather than a sprint.

Visualized as a graph, this type of launch trajectory would show linear growth during the launch period:

Linear Growth

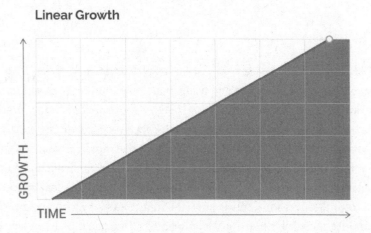

It's slow and steady. Over time, a successful launch would see this trajectory become exponential, once traction picks up and the ripple effects of the smaller steps early on begin to become more pronounced.

Exponential Growth

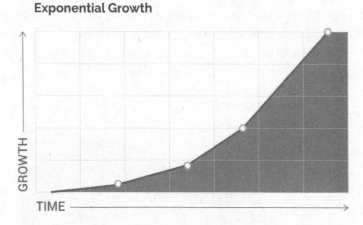

This is how I launched my launch marketing agency, without fanfare and fireworks, simply keeping my head down, working day by day, and seeing steady improvements successfully scale up the business.

The Hare

The Hare launch trajectory is fast and explosive, focused on creating a massive impact on day one and using that momentum to spark sustained growth. An entrepreneur going this route will be zeroed in on the launch day, with the vast majority of pre-launch efforts focusing on maximizing the potential of those first 24 hours. They hope that rapid, early success will put their brand and product name out there instantly (no flying under the radar for creators going this route) and help them to reach big goals quickly.

For these reasons, this is often the route folks take who are crowd-funding their launch, using a platform like Indiegogo or Kickstarter. Crowdfunding campaigns require explosive, early traction in order to get visibility on those platforms and take advantage of the large number of users in those communities.

This is also a favorite of Apple for the release of their latest innovations. They often launch with a bang: long lines outside Apple stories, global launch events, months of anticipation in the lead up, and even the occasional "accidental" leak of a design, event, or date to boost excitement among their loyal followers.

Visualized as a graph, this type of launch trajectory would show logarithmic growth during the launch period:

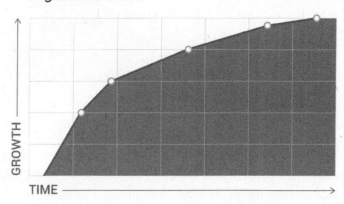

Logarithmic Growth

Traction comes quickly in the beginning, but gains decrease over time. Over time, a successful launch would also see this trajectory become exponential, but there will likely be more fluctuations in the journey. Rather than slow and steady, it's zero to 100 (then back to zero and back up to 100, and so on).

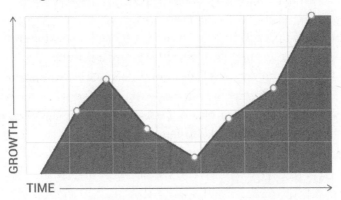

Both the Tortoise and the Hare are powerful and successful launch marketing strategies. Only you can determine which is right for you, but consider a few pros and cons as you make your decision.

The Tortoise Pros & Cons

Pros:

- Ability to minimize inefficiencies in spend (budget/time)
- Production and manufacturing remain manageable, do not get overwhelmed
- Allows you to use profit as your marketing budget from day one

Cons:

- Does not provide big, impressive launch day revenue numbers to quote to media, investors, and other stakeholders

- Requires patience and longer-term thinking
- Does not generally allow for quick, significant strategy pivots

Should be considered by entrepreneurs and creators who:

- Have small budgets and require revenue in order to invest further in their launch strategies
- Have a particularly low tolerance for risk
- Have tight margins and need a laser focus on making each and every marketing effort profitable before scaling up
- Are in the very early stages of product/idea development (for example, a prototype does not exist in any form)
- Are pursuing their idea as a side gig or part-time project, with limited hours available to commit

The Hare Pros & Cons

Pros:

- Can take your product from zero to global hero in a matter of days
- Draws higher levels of interest from investors, media, and other stakeholders
- If you fail fast, you learn fast (and can pivot quickly)

Cons:

- Riskier and more stressful (more pressure for a big, fast, successful launch)
- Can require substantial budget prior to bringing in any revenue
- Becoming a victim of your own success is very real. You are often beholden to production and manufacturing partners, who may be unable to ramp up quickly enough to meet the demand (resulting in unhappy customers).

Should be considered by entrepreneurs and creators who:

- Want to launch through a crowdfunding platform
- Have sizeable budgets that come from sources other than their own launch revenue (e.g., bootstrapping, VCs, angel investors)
- Seek immediate success at launch, due to their need for data to show investors promising data, to capture market share quickly, or to feed their own ego
- Have a higher tolerance for risk
- Have a product or idea ready to go for immediate shipping/delivery to early customers
- Have a comprehensive team alongside them (whether internally or working with external partners) and substantial time/bandwidth to invest in the launch

What Makes People Want Stuff But Change Their Mind?

I've learned the hard way that, in just a matter of seconds, months of hard work, community building, and preparation can come crashing down once the prospective customer reaches the sales page on launch day.

I recall one of my earliest launch campaigns, a fantastic augmented reality product. Preparations for launch went very well, we were bringing in prospective customers at a low cost, and engagement among those prospects around the product was excellent. Folks had responded well to the price point, the founding team, and the product features. We were set for a big launch day!

Yet once we went live, sales were lethargic to say the least. After one week, we knew we were going to fall well short of our revenue goal and canceled the entire launch.

What went wrong?

There was an incongruity between expectation and reality among prospective customers. During the pre-launch marketing stage, the only visual assets we had were of the product itself. Photos showing the product on a white background, for example, or videos showing how the technology worked. These assets had acquired an audience of young adults, with our community consisting of majority 18- to 25-year-old males.

Just one day before launch, the client sent over their live launch campaign multimedia assets. It consisted almost entirely of videography and photography showing tweens and young teenagers using the product.

We knew then that we were in trouble.

The moment the pre-launch audience hit the website and saw children using the product, their interest was gone. A group of young men are very, very unlikely to jump onboard and get excited about a product that appears to be a play toy for a 12-year-old.

Clearly, there was error on both our part and our client's part. A huge miscommunication that had gone unnoticed throughout the pre-launch phase (one that led us to overhaul our client communication methods and, as a consequence, have never seen happen again!). However, put that aside for now and let's consider the effect this incongruity between expectation and reality had on the consumer.

After all, the product hadn't changed. The features, price point, and technology was the same on launch day as it had been in the weeks before. Just 48 hours prior, the pre-launch prospects had been excited, credit cards out and ready to buy. When launch arrived, there had been a dramatic change of heart.

You'll remember from the previous chapter that "wanting stuff" is about the emotional reaction generated by the stuff, how it makes the person feel, rather than about the stuff itself. People want a Ferrari not for the practicality, the mechanics, or the gas mileage. They want it because it makes them feel successful.

The carmaker knows this. They also know their target market is ultra-high-end-growth individuals and that men account for 95 percent of their sales. Their marketing is tuned in to this, with ads full of young, attractive women and insinuations of power, status, and luxury. If Ferrari changed their advertising to start showing pensioners as owners of their car, they'd likely lose the interest of much of their current customer base. Owning the car would no longer make them feel the same way.

Any entrepreneur or creator must make sure that the expectation of their product matches the reality. Any incongruity in expectation will cause a cacophony of problems, particularly in launch marketing.

Whenever I meet someone who finds themselves in this type of situation, one in which they had massive interest that disappeared rapidly, I get asked the same question: how can I get it (or them, the potential customer) back?

Let's be frank—they're deep in quicksand and the odds aren't looking good.

At this stage of a launch, if they've been following the Five-Step High-Profit Launch System in this book, they're long past the time when they can preemptively resolve sales objections and customer concerns. They've spent weeks, if not months, communicating with and engaging their potential customers, worked hard to solve any potential sales hurdles, and their near-term success relies heavily on the group of prospective customers they've built in advance of launch. There isn't much room for error. In many cases the best option is to start over, as painful as that sounds.

In the augmented reality product launch I worked on where we made a huge expectation-reality mistake, the room for error was so slim that we ended up canceling the campaign and shutting the entire launch down. A piece of the puzzle was missing, and we hadn't noticed. By the time we had launched, it was too late to try to find or replace that piece.

If you find yourself in this scenario and are committed to keep moving forward in spite of the incongruity your prospects have experienced, focus on the following:

1. Honesty to rebuild trust
2. Re-prioritizing your current launch plans by understanding what, if anything, *did* work in the misfire

3. Leaning on other brands
4. Adjusting goals and budgets to align with new expectations
5. Move forward like a Stoic

Honesty

If you're an entrepreneur, there will always be new problems where you feel like your back is against the wall. Manufacturing timelines might be delayed, products shipped might be faulty, customer service teams are overwhelmed and slow to respond to queries, or you'll have the honor of an internet stranger criticizing your brand or product across the web.

Whatever the problem, if you're offering a product to consumers, it'll likely result in annoyed customers. In my time working on launches, I've probably seen every problem imaginable and all sorts of responses from the entrepreneur to deal with it.

The worst possible thing you can do is bury your head in the sand. With dozens or more frustrated folks coming at you with complaints, an easy option is to shut down the laptop, ignore the emails, and pretend it's not as bad as it really is. Do not do this. The noise will grow like a snowball from hell and, before you know it, you're faced with a cacophony of anger that can overwhelm you.

Not too long ago, I worked with a founder on the launch of a home goods product who chose this route and suffered the consequences. They missed their shipping date and did a poor job communicating honestly with their customers as to why and what they were doing to get back on track. They skirted around the problem, ducked and dived around providing any sort of genuine answer, and lost customers by the bucketload.

When all was said and done, close to $150,000 in chargebacks and refunds decimated their early success. They were also the recipient of harsh rhetoric online and legal threats. A few memorable quotes included: "I will reach out to the media," "This is a scam," and "I am reporting your company to the FTC." Certainly, these are not comments you want associated with you and your brand.

Another terrible option is to get defensive when potential customers question your legitimacy or the viability of your product. To be fair, it is understandable why some folks will go that route. They've spent months or years creating something and it must feel awful for strangers to be critical without giving your product the time and attention you feel your hard work deserves. However, this approach only exacerbates the problem.

I once had a client launch very successfully, only for some technical skepticism about the product to start coming in a few days into the launch. Rather than responding with empathy, understanding, and an open mind, the client decided to set up a number of fake accounts on a social media platform and started responding to these criticisms from the new, fake accounts, pretending to be another customer!

Well, let's just say that didn't work out well for them. The prospective customers challenging the product's technical claims quickly came to realize these new accounts were actually the entrepreneurs behind the product launch, and the problem spiraled. Rather than facing a few challenging questions from prospective customers, this poor attempt to deceive their community was picked up by other websites and went viral.

Let's consider the opposite, better approach to challenges like these.

When working on the launch of an audio product a few years ago, the entrepreneur behind it missed their shipping date for a section of their customers. As soon as they knew this would happen, they immediately sent an email to customers being honest, transparent, and apologetic. I recall the email started with the phrase "I'm ashamed to be writing this" and ended with "I have no excuses. I'm very sorry." There was also a live-streamed Q&A session where community members could speak directly with the founder and get clarity on the situation. You can't get much more vulnerable than that. The entrepreneur also clearly laid out details on the current problems they were facing with their shipping partner and concrete steps as to what's happening to get back on track.

Do you know what the response was?

Not a single refund. Positive responses came flooding back. Customers applauded the openness and professionalism. The company ended up forging an even stronger bond with their new customers and went on to continued growth and success.

This type of honesty extends throughout a product launch and, in fact, throughout business. If your launch has failed to incite the excitement and interest you'd expected, being honest with your community and using these folks as allies will be important to getting you back on the right track.

One example of this that you can consider are buyer and non-buyer surveys.

For those who *did* convert, a simple one-question survey asking them why gives you valuable feedback that you can integrate into your future marketing for further success. Was it a specific feature? A recurring problem they have that your product solves? Or was it simply because they are your family and would buy anything at any price to support you?

For those that *didn't* convert, a different survey asking them why will offer insight as to what you can do from here. Was it an unexpected cost? Was the product not what they had expected? Was there an issue with the checkout? It doesn't have to be a terribly negative communication. For example, you can send an email highlighting the success of your launch with a simple P.S. at the end for those who have decided not to buy yet. Keep the number of questions to a minimum and leave at least one open-ended question to allow potential customers to provide more detailed feedback. Whatever the reason in their decision not to purchase, you've lost some level of trust that needs to be rebuilt. Honesty, openness, and vulnerability are valuable ways to do this.

Re-prioritizing your launch plans

The online launch world changed dramatically with the birth of crowdfunding. The advent of platforms such as Kickstarter and Indiegogo meant that anyone could put an idea out into the world and potentially get the funding to make it a reality, without investing too much time, money, and energy at the front end of the business. It democratized access to capital and, for the first time, made that access truly global.

In the golden years of crowdfunding, which many put between 2012 and 2016, a lot of crowdfunding campaigners rode the wave of novelty. This was a relatively new and exciting type of consumerism that grabbed the attention of shoppers, early adopters, creatives, and media alike. Crowdfunding campaigns could raise six figures in funding by simply drafting a campaign page and publishing a news release.

The novelty eventually wore off. After some crowdfunding campaigns raised big amounts of capital from a large number of backers yet failed to successfully deliver the product, a wariness emerged. Early adopters weren't so quick to get their credit cards out in support of these projects and media outlets weren't so keen to put these campaigns front and center for their readers.

It took a while for new crowd funders to catch up with this evolution. Creators were still in the mindset that simply creating a neat product was enough. They'd launch a campaign, contact a few media outlets, and assume the money would roll in. Alas, it did not. I experienced one of the direct consequences of this. To this day, many entrepreneurs contact me in desperation, having launched and flopped, looking for answers and wondering what they did wrong.

At this stage of a launch, once the campaign is underway and time is of the essence, a key recommendation is not to dwell on what went wrong. It's often too late for the launch to backtrack and try to fix an error, you can focus on that in a campaign autopsy at a later date. Instead, look at what went right and re-prioritize your launch plans. What, if anything, *did* work? Where *did* customers and funding come from? Oftentimes, in those answers and that data, you can find glimmers of opportunity on which you could build a whole new strategy.

For example, while press outreach may have failed miserably, perhaps a small email list of family, friends, and early interested supporters have converted into customers at a solid rate. If so, could you explore opportunities to further engage that group through referral contests or new offers? Could you look to replicate that strategy again during the live launch campaign with a new list of early supporters, dusting off your Rolodex and digging deep into your LinkedIn network?

With any launch not going to plan, my priority is first to find what's gone right rather than dwell on what went wrong. The immediate action steps need to be about increasing conversions. This will usually come more easily by increasing what you've done right, rather than trying to redo what you've done wrong.

Leaning on other brands

Like an athlete getting caught doping, a failed launch by a brand immediately results in lost credibility. As mentioned above, honesty is one way to rebuild that trust with potential customers. Another way is to piggyback on the credibility of another brand.

Consider this: one promotional email from Kickstarter to their community about a project on their website can generate for that project upward of $20,000 in funding. Sometimes, as much as $50,000—from a single email. This is because the Kickstarter community trusts Kickstarter! The platform has a phenomenal amount of credibility with its members. When Kickstarter promotes a project, they're sharing that credibility with the brand and product being promoted.

In this situation, you're looking for ways that a marketing message to another brand's community can happen in a way that would isolate the customer journey so the customer remains in their existing, trusted ecosystem. For example, creating a unique offer that the brand can present to their community via their own marketing channels, such as an email newsletter sent directly from that brand to their audience. That's the website, brand, and experience they know and love. Don't disrupt it. Instead, lean on it to get through this difficult time for you and your own brand.

Adjusting goals and budgets

As the big launch day approaches, our ambitions start to get even more real. We eat, sleep, and dream about big sales volumes, crowds of happy customers, and viral traction. We can taste success.

This makes adjusting expectations all the more difficult when ambitions don't become a reality. Entrepreneurs have invested so much in the launch—time, money, emotion, and energy—that the notion of adjusting expectations can feel like accepting defeat and acknowledging failure, which many can't bear to contemplate.

If you're anything like me, you hate to be wrong. Earlier this year, I was on a road trip with my wife across the US. We were somewhere in rural Tennessee within just a few miles of our hotel for the night. However, our phone batteries had died after a long day of driving, and we hadn't prepared a map or directions for a no-phone situation.

We rolled up to a T-junction, fields as far as the eye could see on the left and the same on the right. Which way to turn? Before my phone battery had died, I had sworn I saw the map directing us left. My wife believed it to be right. I was the one behind the wheel, so left we went. It was snowing and getting dark as we entered what must have been our ninth or tenth hour driving that day. Getting lost was the last thing we needed. I felt confident in my decision, though. I knew we were close to our hotel; we couldn't go too far wrong.

After taking the turn, we drove for a few minutes. Then, a few more. And a few more after that. I could see my wife's eyes on me. She didn't hold back in letting me know about her skepticism in my sense of direction (or my "location radar," a phrase I fondly recall she shouted at me that day, fumbling over her words due to fatigue and frustration).

I couldn't be wrong. I wouldn't be wrong. This *was* the right way, it had to be.

It wasn't.

Say hello to cognitive dissonance. According to this psychological theory, when two ideas are not psychologically consistent with each other, people do all in their power to change them until they become consistent. After miles driving down a road and no hotel in sight as we passed a sign informing us that we were about to enter Arkansas, the notion that I was correct in my directions was becoming increasingly inconsistent with reality. Yet I persisted until the dissonance was simply too much. I turned around on the empty road and headed back in the opposite direction. My inability to accept my mistake led to an extra 45 minutes or so to what was already a long day of driving—and an angry wife!

Entrepreneurs who face a failed launch can often experience something similar. They've worked so hard for this, surely it cannot fail. They must be right. The problem can't be them, their product, their strategy. It just can't. I've been on calls with entrepreneurs as they experience this and have had to bear the brunt of their frustration as they experience these emotions. It's hard to hear and even harder to experience. Yet, it's this dissonance that they must get past in order to objectively understand the situation they're in and strategically attempt to change the trajectory of their launch.

At this stage, it's time to step back and create a new set of goals, budgets, and expectations. This won't be the campaign they'd hoped for. So, what *can* it be? What does success look like now?

There's no shame in trying and failing. In fact, failing only becomes failure if you give up. If you brush yourself off, get back up, and try again, then you're certainly not a failure. I once worked with an entrepreneur who was launching his third product on Kickstarter. While his second campaign was a six-figure success and his third, the one we were working on, even better, his first campaign had failed. He told me that he doesn't try to hide that campaign and brush it under the rug, unlike many of the entrepreneurs or crowdfunding campaigners who have had a similar experience. Instead, he keeps that first, failed campaign highly visible to him and his team as a reminder to him of the learning curve they have been on and the challenges overcome.

I've also experienced this myself. Before setting up my launch marketing agency, I spent six months trying to launch paid marketing content for the nonprofit world, such as online courses, eBooks, marketing templates, and webinars. Do you know how many customers I had in that six-month period? One. That business effort generated a mere $9, through one customer purchasing an email marketing eBook. After spending half a year creating all sorts of marketing content, all I had to show for it was a library of content I had developed that, quite clearly, nobody wanted!

It was a horrible experience. I was sad and disappointed, and I spent many nights doubting myself and whether I had what it takes to be an entrepreneur. I didn't dwell on it too long, though. While, unlike the aforementioned client, I don't have reminders of this failure so it stays fresh in my mind, I learned from it and have used that experience to move forward.

Let's also put it into perspective—who hasn't failed? New entrepreneurs aren't the only ones who suffer a product launch failure. Consider Google Glass, launched in 2013–2014 to quite the furor and yet failed miserably. Amazon launched their Fire Phone in the summer of 2014 and by the end of summer the following year it had been discontinued. Furthermore, do you remember when McDonald's launched their Mighty Wings—"juicy, bone-in chicken wings in a bold, spicy breading"? No, me neither.

It's at times like this that I may gently remind a struggling entrepreneur of a wonderful Denis Waitley quote: "Failure should be our teacher, not our undertaker. Failure is delay, not defeat. It is a temporary detour, not a dead end."

Move forward like a Stoic

Ever since first coming across Stoicism in my mid-20s, it's been a pillar in my perspective on life. While there are several variants of Stoicism, they all broadly stem from the same concept: an operating system for life that deals with the trials and challenges of the human condition.

A particular principle that has meant a lot to me is one from a famous Stoic, Epictetus. He suggested that it's not *things* that upset us, but *how we think about things*. We can't control what happens around us or to us, but we can control how we think and feel about them.

Like many of you reading this book, as an entrepreneur, I've faced my fair share of unexpected hurdles, frustrations, and failures. Many of these were outside of my control. However, I know that my interpretation of, and response to, these things are within my control, so that's what I try to focus on.

This is true of a failed launch. When a launch goes awry, it's easy to get desperate. Start flailing. Sell your soul to the devil for the hope that things could turn around. The truth is that by the time it occurs, it is often outside of our control. We're too late.

What does a Stoic do with failure? They make the most of it. Marcus Aurelius wrote: "The impediment to action advances action. What stands in the way becomes the way." Too many times I've seen entrepreneurs continue down the same path after a launch failure, exhausting themselves physically, emotionally, and financially.

Rather than dwelling on what's happened, doubling down on what hasn't worked, and digging a deeper hole, take time to stop, pause, and objectively reflect. Fail forward, as many folks say, and turn this bump in the road into your new path of success.

Grandy's Glorious Bakery Launches!

At this stage in the journey of Grandy's Glorious Bakery, launch day has arrived. We've confirmed that a large enough community is eager to tuck in to a new line of baked goods, we've built a list of 500 interested people, and we've delivered them content to ease any concerns they may have had about showing up ready to buy on launch day, either online or physically at the launch event itself. Here's how we made sure this audience converted into customers:

1. Firstly, we ensured the offer met (or exceeded) their expectations. The goodies on display at the launch event came fresh out of the oven, superbly sliced, and delightfully decorated. Pieces of art. Da Vinci himself would have been impressed. We made big signs to ensure launch day pricing and discounts were obvious to anyone walking by.

2. We live-streamed the entire event on our website. A family member, phone in hand, went around showing those who could not attend in-person the beauty of the bakes on sale and the reactions of those enjoying them for the very first time.

3. The layout planning for the garden worked well, with our focus on simplicity and accessibility. The flow of customers was smooth and fluid, with minimal lines or confusion.

4. The same went for our website. Our simple landing page, easy ordering process, and efforts to make the web visitor experience seamless regardless of the device or payment method they used, ensured anyone ordering online was able to without issue.

5. Our request for family and friends to arrive early to the launch event worked as planned. Before the official start time that morning, the garden was buzzing with a dozen or more people drinking coffee, chatting, and enjoying a baked treat. We even had a few cars stop just to see what the excitement was all about!

6. Last but not least, the one and only Grandy was front and center. She welcomed folks into the garden, walked around with samples, took time to speak on camera on our live-stream, and even sneaked an extra (free) cookie or two into customer's orders. Anyone who entered the garden party walked away happy, full, personally connected to the brand, and feeling the experience had surpassed their expectations.

To go one step further, we asked customers for their mailing address, under the pretense that they would be entered into a raffle. In fact, Grandy used this information to send a personal thank-you note to every single customer who purchased on launch day, whether in-person or online. With that one small gesture, she ensured they would be customers for life. Grandy's Glorious Bakery was the talk of the town!

My Favorite Tools

During the audience conversion step, you'll find me using:

- **Unbounce:** Landing page builder for us to design, develop, test, and optimize launch marketing web pages. If we're using a crowdfunding platform to launch, like Kickstarter or Indiegogo, Unbounce would be replaced with the respective platform as our sales page.
- **Shopify/Indiegogo/Kickstarter:** Payment platform to collect customer transactions.
- **Facebook/Instagram Advertising:** My go-to marketing channel for promoting an offer to potential customers and driving them to our landing pages.
- **Google/YouTube Advertising:** A secondary marketing channel for driving web traffic, in addition to Facebook/Instagram advertising.
- **Klaviyo:** Email marketing and SMS marketing platform, where we can collect and communicate with our email and SMS communities.
- **Google Forms:** Simple survey tool to collect answers from prospective customers.
- **Facebook Groups:** Spaces on the Facebook platform that deliver an open and transparent line of communication between founders and potential customers.
- **Google Analytics:** Analytics platform that allows us to evaluate the behavior and performance of our web traffic.
- **Databox:** Analytics dashboard that allows us to collate marketing from different platforms in one, clean view.
- **Adobe Creative Suite:** Software we use for graphic design, video editing, web development, and photography.
- **Google Drive:** My go-to file storage platform where we keep any and every document, PowerPoint, graphic, analysis, and folder created during a launch.

CHAPTER SEVEN

Power Your Profit

N THIS CHAPTER, you'll learn about Scale and Optimize, Step 5 of the Five-Step High-Profit Launch System, including:

- How to drive rapid growth once you've begun converting your target audience into customers
- The two types of e-commerce scale and when to use them
- Getting creative with your growth experiments while sustaining existing success
- Hurdles to rapid growth and how to overcome them

This should be done following completion of the previous chapters (Validation, Audience Acquisition, Audience Engagement, and Audience Conversion), *only* once your pre-launch community is acquired, engaged, and has begun to convert. It is recommended you allow yourself one to three months to complete the strategies in this chapter, depending on the launch trajectory you choose to pursue.

Placerita Canyon and the Forty-Eighters

On March 9, 1842, a chap called Francisco Lopez was among a group looking for lost horses in an area of California that's now known as Placerita Canyon. Upon taking a rest under an oak tree, he fell into a dream in which he found himself floating in a pool of gold, wealthy beyond belief. When he awoke hungry, he pulled some wild onions from the ground nearby and discovered gold flakes clinging to their roots. This is the first verified discovery of gold in California. What followed is what's now known as the California Gold Rush.

Word of the gold spread slowly at first. By 1848, the number of gold-seekers was still in the low thousands but starting to pick up. These prospectors, known as "Forty-Eighters" (the year they arrived in California), found large amounts of easily accessible gold on the surface of the ground. These early arrivals found financial rewards worth 10 to 15 times the daily wage of a laborer on the East Coast of the country. By 1855, the gold was harder to find, and only larger groups of workers could retrieve it profitably. By that time, mining companies were making all the money. Average Joe was out of luck.

Launches face a trajectory akin to the California Gold Rush. When your idea launches, you will have temporary access to early, precious pockets of sales and customer information that will help you make critical decisions on how to grow revenue as quickly as possible. I had one client, for instance, who found "gold" among pilot communities. Pilots had never fallen into the high-priority audience category prior to launch, but sales from that group were growing quickly due to word of mouth. We tweaked our strategies to market more toward this nugget of gold and reaped the rewards.

These golden pockets of sales and data are most visible during the launch period, which can usually last from as little as one day to a few months. This means even the longest launch period is a short amount of time in the lifecycle of a business, and, like the Forty-Eighters, you must rush to make the most of this short period and find your gold.

Knowing there's gold out there is critical, but you also have to know how to look. To that, I offer a piece of advice a mentor gave me long ago: "Look for impact, not increment."

You are better off spending your time finding one vast reserve of gold than moving from river to river in search of flakes. In the context of your marketing efforts for a new business launch, this means trying things that can result in significant sales improvements rather than small progressions. Changing one sentence halfway down a web page may improve your sales marginally, but it's unlikely to be a gamechanger. Changing the price of a product to be more appealing to a wider base of potential customers often makes massive positive changes in your sales and revenue. If a company increased the cost on their website of their $90 product by 10 percent (up to $99) while maintaining the same conversion rate of website visitors into customers, 100 customers would generate an additional $900 in revenue. At scale (after one year, two years, five years etc.), this would be a huge win for the company.

Once you've kicked off your sales and started to bring real revenue in, it's time to add fuel to the fire. It's time to find this gold and, in e-commerce marketing terminology, scale.

Scale is part of the fifth step in the Five-Step High-Profit Launch System. But what does this really mean?

The Merriam-Webster dictionary suggests that "scale," in a business sense is: "increasingly being used as shorthand for 'scale up' (to grow or expand in a proportional and usually profitable way)." For others, it means to get incrementally more results with the same inputs (more profitability as you grow).

For this launch version of the concept, I consider it more like Merriam-Webster. A way of proportionally growing. It doesn't necessarily mean you must increase profitability as you grow, but you must at least maintain profitability. For me and the launch concepts I teach, "unprofitable scale" would be an oxymoron. (Notably, for many startup companies that have investors, it's not an oxymoron but is in fact an expectation. As risk-averse entrepreneurs, unprofitable scale is not a path we like to take.)

When ramping up, there are two types of scale I tend to look at: vertical scale and horizontal scale.

With vertical scaling ("scaling up"), you're adding more power to your existing areas of success. For example, if you've launched and found your gold in one particular demographic of customers, vertical scaling would be about putting more power (more time, money, investment) into this particular area.

With horizontal scaling ("scaling out"), you achieve more power by adding new areas of opportunity to your strategies, sharing the growth across many. An example of this would be finding success in one country and rolling out your strategy across many new countries.

Both are valuable. While vertical is easier, horizontal is where the extensive scale can occur, given it takes a lot longer to hit a ceiling on opportunity. Consider if you see success in women, 35 to 55 years old, living in metropolitan areas in the United States. You can certainly invest more resources to find more customers of that demographic and successfully grow. Eventually, however, you're going to come up against a wall and start getting diminishing returns. There simply aren't that many easily accessible potential customers in that audience segment. If, instead of doubling down on the US market, you choose to scale horizontally and launch similar strategies to the UK, Canada, Australia, and the European Union, you're immediately tapping into a bigger pool of potential customers.

When I helped to launch Tempest, a revolutionary personal weather system, and helped the creator, WeatherFlow, raise $2.1 million during that launch period and another $2.5 million in the months that followed, it was critical to maximize both forms of scale. During the core launch campaign period, the company had shipping available only to folks in the US (as is often the case for many US-based entrepreneurs, for whom US shipping is much easier to deliver on than having to deal with customs, import, shipping, and VAT fees internationally). This one-country focus meant vertical scale was the route to go. There are only so many early-adopter meteorologists (their key target audience) to tap into, and continuing to scale up with that group into the millions of dollars in revenue was no mean feat.

A few months in, it was a delight to hear they were finally able to expand beyond the US, even if it was just to one additional country,

Canada. The ability to expand our scale efforts horizontally, as well as vertically, increased the return on investment of our strategies immediately from a 5x return to a 13x return.

A launch could and should be a combination of both vertical and horizontal scale (as long as both are applicable to the offer being presented). Keep in mind, though, that horizontal, more often than not, will offer the biggest bang for your buck.

HIIT Launch

Sebastian Coe is a former British track and field athlete. He was a big name in the 1970s and 1980s, when he won four Olympic medals and set nine outdoor and three indoor world records in middle-distance track events. The most prominent period of his success was a now-famous 41-day period in 1979, in which he set three world records: completing an 800-meter race in 1:42.33, a mile in 3:48.95, and the 1500 meter in 3:32.03. Put simply, the very best in his field during his time.

He was also one of the first well-known athletes to train using HIIT (high-intensity interval training). This is a form of exercise alternating short periods of intense anaerobic exercise with less intense recovery periods. Studies have shown HIIT to lead to significantly improved cardiovascular fitness, increased weight loss, reduced blood sugar, improved oxidation levels, and better cognitive performance.

If you're a gym goer or active individual, you see HIIT everywhere these days. SoulCycle, CrossFit, and Peloton are all now household names based, in part, due to many folks having been attracted by a high-intensity type of activity. The rise of HIIT has been a bit of a game-changer in the exercise industry, and I like to apply the same type of high-intensity strategies in our launch concepts, too.

Just like with exercise (and, frankly, with life) you can't be at high intensity all the time during a launch. Don't get me wrong, a launch campaign will always be intense and exhausting. There's little time to put your feet up. However, you should think of your launch trajectory as a high-intensity workout—a longer period of energy and excitement spattered with short bursts of traction, to help maintain the overall positive trajectory.

I also like to compare launches to EKG machines, the medical devices that record how often and how regularly the heart beats. Often-times, you'll see these in movies with the "beep…beep…beep" sound. On a graph, these "beeps" translate into spikes in the y-axis, which is a similar pattern to how you'll often see your revenue tracking during a launch.

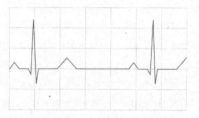

Such bursts of promotion, traction, and energy should be a prior-ity throughout the launch period. These bursts inject new life into the campaign and ensure it concludes with a bang rather than a whimper. Without such bursts of intensity, a launch trajectory can easily lose power and peter out.

Let's consider four tactics to create these bursts of intensity for launches:

1. Reward Releases

A reward release is when you launch additional rewards and offers throughout your launch period, based on the success trajectory. For example, once 500 units are sold, you may release an additional acces-sory or bonus offer. This serves two purposes:

1. It provides a reason to continue communicating with your community through the launch and bringing them to view your offer(s).

2. It presents an opportunity to generate additional revenue/traction from audience members you've already converted into customers.

2. Foot-in-the-Door Upsells

Research suggests that the probability of selling to a new prospect is 5 percent to 20 percent, while the probability of selling to an existing customer is 60 percent to 70 percent.[1] Put simply, it's much easier to sell to an existing customer than to a new prospect.

Use this to your advantage by holding back elements of the offer or adding new components until the first sale has already been made. This is also a great way to make use of any of the feedback you collected during pre-launch from your audiences. Perhaps there were a lot of requests for an additional feature—why not try to incorporate that post-launch and release the new offer back to the audience members who requested it? It's a great way to incorporate earliest supporters into the product journey.

3. Limited Time Promotions

Everyone loves a promotion. Running very limited time (24 to 48 hours) promotions during your launch, such as a heavy discount, seasonal celebration, free gift, VIP access, or affiliate opportunities are great ways to breathe new life into a slowing launch trajectory.

4. Notable Announcements

I always like to save a couple of big announcements until a launch campaign is already up and running. Perhaps it's a partnership with a well-known brand, press from a big media outlet, recommendation from a famous face, or a prestigious award. Announcements like this provide a burst of energy and excitement among both customers and prospects alike.

The Sandbox Strategy

As children (and adults if you fancy it, I suppose), a sandbox is a place to play. A place to create. A place to imagine, build, and shape ideas, risk-free.

In recent decades, the term has been applied to computer programming. A sandbox in this context is an isolated testing environment that enables users to run programs without affecting the application, system, or platform on which they run. For example, software developers use sandboxes to test new programming code on a website before actually pushing that code live onto the site for the public to see.

When I launched the Five-Step High-Profit Launch System, I took the liberty of giving this term a definition and context specific for launch marketers. For launch marketing, a sandbox is an isolated testing environment that enables launch marketers to experiment with new strategies, creative, and positioning, with minimal damage to the performance of the overall campaign. A sandbox is the answer to a question I am often asked by entrepreneurs new to marketing: how much of our spend/focus should be on experiments to find new opportunities and how much of our spend/focus should be on improving the things that we already know work?

For me, the balance should be 80/20. Eighty percent of your time, budget, and attention should be spent on scaling up the things that work, while the remaining 20 percent can be used exploring new ideas.

When I started with WeatherFlow (and their launch of Tempest, the personal weather system) they were already an existing company with successful strategies in place. They weren't looking for a marketing partner for rapid validation or to build preliminary marketing foundations. They were coming looking for growth above and beyond what they could achieve by themselves. This launch was a great example of how to enact the sandbox strategy and WeatherFlow, as an existing company with a stellar reputation and top-notch products, was the perfect brand to use such a method.

With foundations and data we could review, optimize, and double down on 80 percent of the advertising budget went on building upon the strategies that we already knew worked well for the brand. With horizontal and vertical scale tactics, we created new advertising campaigns that accelerated, fine-tuned, and improved the things that were already working for them. By putting 80 percent in things we knew could deliver strong results, we knew we could maintain a high-level of return on investment regardless of how the remaining budget performed. Any less than 80 percent and we risked the possibility of failed sandbox experiments being too damaging to our overall campaign results.

With the remaining 20 percent, we created our sandbox campaigns. For the digital marketing data geeks out there, this is where a lot of the fun is. No idea is a bad idea in the sandbox. As long as a hypothesis is founded on evidence or cohesive theory, anything goes.

Want to run an ad experiment in which the advertiser "forgets" to complete their company's copywriting draft document correctly and an ad goes live with the headline [Insert headline here]?

No problem. (Yes, we really did that. And yes, it worked quite well!)

Want to run an ad experiment in which you purposely misspell the company name in order to gain high-engagement and referrals?

Sure. (Yes, we did that, too, and the results were great.)

Adding to the fact that it's fun to get creative like this, the sandbox strategy has also proven to be a goldmine for us and our clients time and again.

While, by the mid-1850s, the opportunity to head to California in search of gold had come to an end for the average Joe, the fast success of the previous decade stimulated economic growth around the world and presented a plethora of new opportunities. Work on the First Transcontinental Railroad began, partly financed by profits from the California Gold Rush. Farmers in Chile found a new market for their food. Overseas manufactured goods were in high demand. In fact, while traversing the California coast, Australian prospector Edward Hargraves saw similarities between the geography of California and his home country, Australia. He returned to his homeland to discover gold and spark the Australian gold rushes. Historians place the end date for the Australian rushes at 1914—a whopping sixty-three years of additional, mass discoveries of gold.

This is how launch marketing scale and sandbox strategies can work. Success and opportunity lead to new ideas, which leads to further success and opportunity, which again leads to new ideas. It's a chain reaction and helps sustain marketing campaign success over a long period of time.

While my 80/20 suggestion is a nice rule of thumb, it isn't set in stone. Consider a balance that works for you by understanding how much you can risk without impairing the overall success of the campaign. Like many folks in investing say: don't risk what you can't afford to lose.

Overcoming Growth Goblins

Whenever launch marketing strategies start to grow, there are going to be obstacles. I call these growth goblins. Goblins are mischievous and so are these obstacles. I like to create an image of goblins gobbling up growth. Making a mockery of it makes it easy to remember and takes the edge off of the very real frustrations they cause.

Over the years, I've faced and overcome every growth goblin a launch can present. In Chapter Six, we talked about "absence blindness" and how the role of an effective launch manager is predicting customer sales objections and resolving them in advance of the launch. The same principle applies here. It's experience that enables experts to make more accurate predictions on what the goblins might be—and prepare a strategy to overcome them before they rear their ugly heads.

As with absence blindness, through this book my experience is now yours. We can look back to the launches I've completed and prepare you for a handful of common growth challenges together.

Growth Goblin 1: Failing to understand the role of each step in your funnel

Like a chain, a sales funnel is only as strong as its weakest link. If one step in your funnel has problems, the whole thing can fail. There is only so much the other steps can do to take on the responsibility.

Consider a water hose with a hole right in the middle. It doesn't matter how well the rest of the hose is designed, that one hole will prevent water from passing through from one end to the other. Pumping up the water pressure might help a little. Perhaps, with a strong enough flow, *some* water will get past the hole and make it out the other end, but that will only work to a small extent. The water pressure can only take on so much responsibility in solving the problem. Ultimately, that hole needs to be fixed for the hose to work effectively.

The same is true of a sales funnel. Each component of the funnel must be effective for the whole thing to deliver results. Depending on which resource you look at, there are usually between three and eight steps to most sales funnels. We'll keep it simple and consider a funnel as three core steps:

1. Awareness: generating awareness of an offer among a target audience, such as running ads. You may also see this called TOF (Top of Funnel).
2. Consideration: converting awareness into interest, such as a potential customer engaging with the ad in some way and considering the offer you present. You may also see this called MOF (Middle of Funnel).
3. Decision: converting interest into a buying decision. You may also see this called BOF (Bottom of Funnel).

In Chapter 3, we looked at a couple of different funnels (the 1 Percent Funnel and the Fake Checkout Funnel). Let's break our 1 Percent Funnel down into the three steps above:

The 1 Percent Funnel example:

Awareness: To start the funnel, you show your target audience a marketing message.

- Run ads via Facebook/Instagram that show your product and the solution it offers to the user.

Consideration: Those who show interest are shown a specific offer (or offers).

- Those who click on an ad (show interest/engagement) are taken to a web page (which you can set up easily with landing page platforms such as Unbounce, ClickFunnels, or KickOff Labs), where they have the option to sign up by submitting their email address to access deals when your product launches.

Decision: Those who take up the primary offer(s) are pushed to make a bigger commitment.

- Those who sign up are taken to a second web page (moving further down the funnel), where you give them the option to pay 1 percent of the launch price and get guaranteed access to the biggest launch discount.

You might be looking at the above and asking: "Will, where's the actual product purchase?" You're right to ask. These validation funnels are part of a larger launch funnel. When we look at these validation funnels in isolation, the final step (BOF) is to show some level of purchase intent. If we were to place these into the bigger launch funnel, there would be more steps and, as you may have guessed, one of the latter funnel steps would be the product purchase. Similar to a deck of presentation slides, in which one slide can both stand alone with a message and purpose, while also being part of the wider presentation, small funnels can be added on top of each other like Lego to create something larger.

With the 1 Percent Funnel in mind, let's revisit the role each step has and how just one issue within one step can cause the funnel to collapse.

Top of Funnel Awareness

In validation, top of the funnel awareness comes from advertising and driving traffic to a web page. A key concern here is the cost of that traffic. For example, if the cost to advertise to certain audiences is high, all your funnel metric costs will likely be high. Similarly to how gas prices rise for you and me when costs rise for the gas companies, if the cost to reach people is high, then the cost per ad click is also high and the cost of each visitor signing up on the page is high. High costs get passed on.

At the top of the funnel, the priority is to bring in quality traffic at the lowest cost. Two levers we can pull to affect this in our validation funnels are: (a) finding more affordable audiences to show ads (lower cost to show ads will lead to lower costs down the funnel), and (b) increasing the rate at which people engage with your ad (Facebook/Instagram ads are billed to the advertiser based how many impressions they receive, so the advertiser will pay the same amount regardless of whether 1 person clicks or 100 people click).

Understanding (and being effective) at this step of your funnel means finding the highest quality traffic at the lowest possible cost. You can control this cost through how you get your message in front of your audience and the rate at which the audience engages with your message.

Middle of Funnel Consideration

At the consideration stage, we're looking for web visitors to sign up on the landing page. A key concern here is the rate at which web page visitors take the step of signing up (rather than leaving the page without taking action). For example, a page that fails to successfully present the offer to the audience will convert visitors into sign-ups at a poor rate. If you receive 100 visitors to the page and have paid (per the previous step of the funnel) a certain amount of money to receive that traffic/awareness, your cost per sign-up will be much lower if you convert 30 of those visitors into sign-ups versus if you convert just three.

Optimizing your web page, by positioning your offer in the best possible way and making the user experience as seamless as possible, is the lever you can pull to ensure this step of your funnel is a strong link in the chain.

Bottom of Funnel Decision

At the decision stage of the 1 Percent Funnel, we're looking for web visitors to make a small purchase (1 percent of the product price). A key concern here is the rate at which people who have shown interest in your product idea (by signing up in the previous step) have real purchase intent behind their interest. Is it something they will actually pay money for, or is it an idea they like, but their interest is not strong enough to make them want to buy? Someone might see you're launching a product idea and they sign up to register interest. However, when they get to this next stage and see the price point/more information on the commitment they would need to make, they get turned off and leave the page.

If this stage is the hole in your funnel, the message is clear: people like your idea but do not agree with how you value it. Perhaps it's the price point or the way you've presented the offer (such as your photos or videos). As excited as they were about the concept, when it comes down to getting their credit card out, you didn't do enough to convince them. While all funnel steps have holes that can make or break the funnel, this is perhaps the most important, and a poor conversion rate of interest into purchase intent shows that the product offer is unlikely to work in its current form.

Growth Goblin 2: Failing to diversify or adapt your team

Most folks creating a business or launching an idea wear all the hats early on. Website building, copywriter, creative director, CEO, engineer, bookkeeper, receptionist, customer service rep—the list goes on. You've possibly been all of these things and more. The reality is: you can't do everything. A lot of early-stage entrepreneurs fall into the trap of being penny-wise and pound-foolish. Founders want to do everything themselves in order to keep costs down. Be careful not to go to an extreme.

I recall one launch in which the solo founder didn't sleep for close to 48 hours over launch day and the day after launch due to the sheer volume of tasks he had to complete and customer service questions to which he had to respond. He was so exhausted he ended up needing to take the next few days off entirely, which most certainly impacted his early traction and launch success.

Another time, we had a client assure us that they could handle community management of their launch Facebook Group. Yet it never became a priority for them and ended up at the bottom of their to-do list each day, often being usurped by another task. The consequence of this was a poorly engaged community, which led to missed revenue once the launch took place.

If you're planning to grow through digital advertising, hire a digital marketing expert. If you're planning to grow through local events, hire an expert event planner. If you want to run a comprehensive launch strategy, make sure each critical component has someone with the time and expertise to manage it. Failing to invest in your team early on can prove to be a huge hindrance to the speed with which you can scale.

Growth Goblin 3: Lacking processes and procedures

There's a famous study you may have heard of that concluded that daily flossing can add 6.4 years to your life expectancy. Like me, you might have asked: what's flossing got to do with living longer?

Many have suggested that this is a case of correlation not implying causation. Sure, people who floss daily live longer but not *because* they floss. Simply, people who floss daily are likely to be the type of people who may be steadfast with their health in all areas of their life.

Whenever my company is hired to take over a brand's launch marketing strategies from another marketing agency, one of the first things I want to know is the level of expertise the other agency has. This allows me to quickly make a call on what strategies have likely been tried and which haven't, without having to dig deep into strategy docs and data.

Do you know what I look for? Naming conventions.

For example, do they have a system for how they label creative assets? How do they structure their client's marketing files? How do they name their ad campaigns?

Why do I do this? Because an agency that has comprehensive, logical, and explicit naming conventions will no doubt display experience and excellence in other areas. Good naming conventions show experience, organization, and a process-focused strategy. If I see a top-notch naming convention system when I look in the ad account, I can be fairly confident the prior agency had run some pretty advanced marketing strategies for the client. Those that don't do naming conventions will likely have implemented strategies with less expertise and cohesion.

Naming conventions don't cause successful launches. However, a marketing agency with excellent naming conventions is likely to be excellent in other areas of their work, too.

Apply this to your own launch. When you're on your own writing out an idea on the back of a napkin, you don't need a process for how your marketing team communicates with your customer service team on prospective customer objections to that idea. When you look to scale, success will seep through such operational cracks like water through a broken bucket. Effective, cohesive processes are a critical foundation for scale.

Growth Goblin 4: Underestimating customer service

Life's easier before you launch for one huge reason: you have no customers to deal with! Once a launch is underway and people are buying whatever you're selling, you've now got an entirely new role to fill.

And it's time-consuming. Research shows that 88 percent of customers expect a response from your business within one hour, while 30 percent expect a response within 15 minutes or less. Day or night. Weekday or weekend.

Never is this more important than when you first launch. After all, depending on how you launch your product, many of your earliest customers will be having their first experiences with your brand through your customer service, not the product itself. In crowdfunding, for example, campaign backers often have a relationship with a brand for months before they try the product. The success of a launch hinges not on the quality of the product (which the customer may not have received yet) but on the strength of your customer service response. I've never seen this done better than by Colin McIntosh, founder and CEO of Sheets & Giggles, the sustainable bedding brand introduced earlier in this book. Sure, their bed sheets are great—sinfully soft, warm in winter, and cool in summer. But his crowdfunding backers didn't have the product yet and didn't know that. It was his passion and commitment to customer service that allowed him to successfully launch his brand in the super-competitive bedding industry.

Dealing with customers will quickly become a full-time role for at least one person. Don't let this come as a surprise. Whether you're a one-person show working out of your garage or a multi person team, any time spent trying to get up to speed with your customer service efforts will be taking away from a focus on growth. Be prepared.

Growth Goblin 5: Focusing only on acquiring new customers

Acquiring a new customer costs a lot more than getting an existing customer to make an additional purchase, with some studies suggesting a new customer can cost five times more.[2] Existing customers are a huge source of revenue, both in terms of purchasing the same product multiple times (for a friend or family member) or cross-selling a customer with another product (a brand offering someone who bought a computer screen the chance to purchase other computer accessories, such as a keyboard, mouse, or hard drive, too). Yet many entrepreneurs focus entirely on converting prospects into new customers and not the low-hanging fruit of generating more revenue from folks who have already converted (or are in the process of converting, such as presenting a bundle accessory offer once a customer is checking out).

There are a few useful ways to maximize growth through re-engaging existing customers:

1. **Involve them in the process**
    As simple as it sounds, if you want to know what people want, you just need to ask. There's no better group to ask for input on new accessories or additional product bundles than the folks who already know and trust you. Tap into your customers to help direct new products and ideas.

2. **Getting the timing right**
    Whether you get a yes or a no when you ask someone for something often depends on timing. If you ask a friend to help you move, doing it right after a compliment would be a better strategy than after a criticism. This is true in launch marketing, too.
    Another example that might ring a bell for you is a psychological tactic introduced by Freedman and Fraser in 1966 called "foot-in-the-door" technique. This is a compliance strategy that assumes if you ask someone for something small, it's then easier to get them to agree to a

bigger ask. For example, asking someone to sign a petition before ask-ing them to donate, rather than simply asking for the donation right away, increases the likelihood that they will agree to it.

When launching a product, the opportunity to increase revenue from existing customers will likely come in two places: the checkout flow or a specific period of calendar time that holds relevance to the customer.

If you buy something online, you'll often see a marketing mes-sage at some point during the transaction that says something along the lines of "you might also like…" or "customers who bought X also bought Y." Perhaps it's as you're viewing the product, about to check-out, or right after completing the purchase. In this scenario, the brand has got their foot in the door with the customers, and now's the time to ask them to commit to something extra.

The calendar also presents opportunities for increasing customer revenue, particularly for launch campaigns. As a launch period comes to an end, I always like to suggest entrepreneurs reach out again to their earliest customers with a special offer whereby they can purchase an addi-tional product for a family or friend, with an exclusive discount but only before the launch period ends. The urgency around the conclusion of the launch period can drive folks to jump on such an offer. Seasonal promo-tions, too, are a great strategy for increasing sales among existing custom-ers. Black Friday, for example, is a fantastic opportunity most brands take advantage of, using limited-time deals to acquire new customers and also to incentivize current customers to come back and buy more.

3. **Presenting the right incentives**

Finally, this brings us to the right incentives. To get a customer to hand over *more* than they had originally planned requires the right encouragement. Discounts and deals are one way to do this. You might also think back to Chapter 4 and what makes people want stuff, when we introduced the concept of socialization (seeing that other people want something makes us more likely to want it too) and scarcity (tap-ping into the fear of missing out). Presenting an offer as exclusive to existing customers, limited in availability, and made available due to overwhelming demand, are all small tactics that, combined, can help make your offer irresistible.

Grandy Grows Her Business

Let's pay Grandy's Glorious Bakery another visit. Following her successful launch day, it was time for Grandy to start building her business in earnest and grow it into a long-term, money-making machine. The launch discount she offered early customers lasted a full two weeks. This gave us that much time to find critical information, such as which products offered the most profit and who our main customers were, enabling us to adjust our marketing for maximum impact. Here's how we took this next step:

1. We studied the numbers from our launch day, looking for gold. We noticed that throughout the validation, pre-launch, and launch day itself, two bakes were by far the most popular: Grandy's coffee cake and her coconut jam pastries. This is gold. We also learned from the customer address information we collected at checkout that a higher percentage of overall customers than we expected were coming from a small town 10 miles away. These customers also spent more, on average, than everyone else. This too, is gold.

2. We researched community events in our gold town 10 miles away and found three events coming up that seemed like sales opportunities for Grandy's Glorious Bakery. We contacted those in charge of these events, asked if we could set up a bake sale, and got a yes from two of the three.

3. For the next two weeks, Grandy focused her baking on the two top-performing products. Yes, it disappointed a few folks who wanted the other bakes, but a business at this stage can't be everything to everybody. By prioritizing, we were able to

maximize the happiness we delivered to our customer base while maximizing Grandy's profit.

4. In addition to the events at the gold town, we restarted our Facebook ad campaign and web page. Instead of the broad approach we used in the validation step, we zeroed our advertising in on the gold town, switched our content to show just the top performers (Grandy's coffee cake and coconut jam pastries) and changed the action we requested on the web page from "sign up" to "buy."

5. Finally, we contacted all the customers from launch day who had paid us a visit from our gold town and let them know of our upcoming attendance at their local events, asking them to stop by and bring a friend.

By focusing our efforts on finding more gold and maximizing the impact of the gold we'd already found, we had an extremely successful launch fortnight. Grandy had quickly grown her launch day success into a fully successful two-week launch period. Good work, Grandy!

My Favorite Tools

During the Scale and Optimize step, you'll find me using:

- **Unbounce:** Landing page builder for us to design, develop, test, and optimize launch marketing web pages. If we're using a crowdfunding platform to launch, like Kickstarter or Indiegogo, Unbounce would be replaced with the respective platform as our sales page.
- **Shopify/Swell/Indiegogo/Kickstarter:** Preorder/sales platforms to collect customer transactions.
- **Facebook/Instagram Advertising:** My go-to marketing channel for promoting an offer to potential customers and driving them to our landing pages.
- **Google/YouTube Advertising:** A secondary marketing channel for driving web traffic, in addition to Facebook/Instagram advertising.
- **TikTok/SnapChat/Reddit/Pinterest Advertising:** A tertiary marketing channel for driving web traffic, in addition to Facebook/Instagram and Google/YouTube advertising.
- **Klaviyo:** Email marketing and SMS marketing platform, where we can collect and communicate with our email and SMS communities.
- **Facebook Groups:** Spaces on the Facebook platform that deliver an open and transparent line of communication between founders and potential customers.
- **Billo App:** Video platform for user-generated video ad creation.
- **Klarna:** Payment platform that offers pay after delivery options and installment plans.
- **Proof:** Website application to build visitors' trust, create urgency, and increase conversions.
- **Google Analytics:** Analytics platform that allows us to evaluate the behavior and performance of our web traffic.

- **Databox:** Analytics dashboard that allows us to collate marketing from different platforms in one, clean view.
- **Adobe Creative Suite:** Software we use for graphic design, video editing, web development, and photography.
- **Google Drive:** My go-to file storage platform where we keep any and every document, PowerPoint, graphic, analysis, and folder created during a launch.

CHAPTER EIGHT

What Happens Now?

HOWEVER SUCCESSFUL A launch, no business is immune to growth stagnation. I've seen it many times, particularly in the period directly following a big launch promotion. After a phenomenal launch and initial surge in interest, an entrepreneur sees their growth slow down. It may even die off completely and result in "zero-dollar days"—full 24-hour periods when not a single sale comes in. Entrepreneurs are left stunned, seeing their traction go from boom to bust so quickly.

As you close out your launch period, you must start to think about longevity. At launch, many folks want glamor. They want the million-dollar day one and a sky-rocketing trajectory. To achieve this, they pursue strategies that prioritize the quickest and easiest results (the most accessible gold in Chapter 7). I have no criticism of this; it's a perfectly viable way to achieve early success.

In the long run, you can't rely on this low-hanging fruit. After all, there is only so much fruit to pick before you need to reach for the higher branches. In the stage after your launch period, growing your business with strategies that drive incremental success—step by step, piece by piece, day by day (moving up one branch at a time)—is the way to go. Congratulations! You have entered the stage of long-term business ownership.

After your launch success, the questions you ask yourself change. You've started a business, now you have to maintain it. How can you make (and keep) customers happy? How can you maintain a steady, growing stream of sales coming in? How can you incentivize your first customers to tell their friends? How can you manage cash flow? How can you find more customers from further afield? Changes at this stage often start small. And, over time, these small increments of improvement add up. Think of it like compound interest, which has a power of historic proportions.

On June 3, 1789, as Benjamin Franklin neared the end of his life, he amended his will to donate $1,000 to his native city, Boston, and another $1,000 to his adopted city, Philadelphia. There was just one catch: Franklin placed each sum in a fund that would serve the designated purpose of supporting the public good and gather interest for a period of 200 years. In 1990, Franklin's Boston endowment was worth more than $5 million, and his Philadelphia fund about half of that.

This is the value of compound interest. With enough time, a thousand dollars becomes millions. The growth of those funds on a daily basis looks immaterial. Over longer periods of time, the growth is astronomical.

The same can be said of growing your online sales. Long-term, to create a constant and growing flow of sales, you'll need to see a bigger picture and look beyond the horizon. The truth to online growth and sustainability is that incremental gains add up and the key to this growth lies in the details. It's all about making small changes over time rather than sweeping changes too quickly—quite the contrast to the launch marketing tactics we discussed in earlier chapters. Over time, these incremental improvements provide impactful marketing gains.

Imagine working to improve your sales performance by just 1 percent every day. That's nothing. However, just a 1 percent improvement, every day, will result in a 37-times overall improvement over the course of a year. Zappos famously promoted this 1 percent rule to employees as a method for personal improvement. James Clear, author of *Atomic Habits*, is a proponent of using it for habit-forming. Similarly, Jeff Bezos refers to it when discussing Amazon's growth strategy, and the former UFC fighter Benson Henderson used it to guide his training.

In the context of growing your business through marketing, incremental success might mean testing new creative materials to get more people to click on your ads, a minor tweak to your sales page, or improving the number of people who open your marketing emails by changing the time of day you schedule those emails to go out. As you build out your long-term marketing strategy and implement those efforts, the results compound. Furthermore, your brand develops, your processes improve, and your foundations on which to deliver results grows stronger. Assets you had no access to prior to launch, such as brand recognition or advertising data, begin to play an additional role in the compounding growth of your results. Slowly but surely, your marketing efforts get easier, cheaper, and more effective. Another way of considering this is the Flywheel effect, a concept developed in the book *Good to Great*. The author, Jim Collins, shares how it is momentum, over time, that can generate monumental transformations. He notes how each turn of a heavy flywheel builds upon work done earlier, compounding your investment of effort, bit by bit, turn by turn. This is how entrepreneurs can view their marketing efforts once the fireworks and short-term traction of a launch marketing strategy are starting to wind down.

In every area of your business and with every hat you wear as a founder, there will always be opportunities to improve, however slight they may feel. Learning, testing, and validating does not end with a successful launch. This is only the beginning. Post-launch, be like Franklin. Focus on compound interest and incremental improvements. That's the route to sustainable growth.

Transitioning the Five-Step System from Launch to Longevity

The lessons you've learned throughout this book have been a part of a comprehensive five-step system for you to launch your business, but they apply to long-term business success as well.

- Validation isn't done and dusted once your product has been proven.

- Finding new prospective customers doesn't end with your first few sales.
- Scale shouldn't come to an abrupt halt after you've hit your five-, six-, or seven-figure goals.

This system is cyclical, and the steps are continuous. Think of it as an Olympic running track. Sure, each loop has a start and an end, but they are one and the same. There is always more track to run.

Always be validating

All testing is validation. While earlier chapters spoke of validation as a way to prove or disprove the market fit for an idea of a product offer, it extends to any idea.

Do you think you might get better marketing results by adding a wider variety of acquisition channels? Could you see happier, healthier, and more productive employees with a remote-first workplace? Maybe you want to boost brand credibility with a public relations push?

At this stage of your journey, think of validation not as a starting point but as a critical component in everything you do. Have an idea, create your hypothesis, and set out to prove or disprove that hypothesis. Some will succeed, others will fail. With every validation, you take a small step forward.

Continue to identify, acquire, engage, and convert new audiences

Your pre-launch community of prospective customers tend to convert, at launch, into customers within a range of 3 percent to 8 percent. For every 100 prospective customers you acquire into your wider community (like an email list), 3 to 8 of them will become a customer almost immediately when you present them with the chance to buy.

In the months following launch, you'll see your conversion rate of these prospective customers increase as you generate more brand awareness and credibility. For the clients I work with, I tend to see a conversion rate double in the months following the big launch. For example, if you saw a 5 percent conversion rate of your community during your launch month, an analysis six-months down the line may show roughly another 5 percent of your pre-launch community has purchased your product.

While that's a nice bump, it emphasizes just how critical it is to keep working on growing your audiences. After all, roughly 95 percent of people who show interest in your offer by becoming a member of your community won't buy at launch and, even once your brand is up and running, there are still around 90 percent of your community who won't commit to the purchase.

Like a leaky bucket, you have to keep filling your community up. If you don't, the water (your audience of prospective customers) will eventually dry up and the flow (of sales) will come to a halt. You may have heard this referred to in marketing or sales terms as "filling the funnel." Marketers need to keep filling their marketing funnel and moving prospective customers through each step of the funnel in order to maintain traction.

In addition, never stop learning from those in your funnel—from both happy and unhappy customers alike, as well as those who are not yet customers. Keep asking questions that can provide insight on what they like about what you're selling, what they dislike, and what would make them like it more. Discover how customers are using the product in their everyday lives and what could be done to improve that experience. Continue to understand and resolve the sales objections they may be facing.

At this stage in your journey, if everything has gone to plan, you have access to something magical for the first time: happy customers. With this, you can add a new stage to your marketing funnel and a whole new dimension to your acquisition and engagement strategies— customer advocacy and retention.

There are a few ways that customer advocacy and retention create this new dimension:

1. **Word-of-mouth marketing.** Whether it's an off-the-cuff comment from a customer to a friend during a dinner or a full-fledged affiliate platform for your biggest fans, there is no greater tool in your marketing toolbox than having your supporters sell your product for you. As soon as you've shipped your products and satisfied your customers, get to work on making their post-purchase glow work for you in acquiring new prospects and customers.

2. **Credibility.** Finally, you have products out in the market. This means that you also now have a chance to start building online reviews. While usually not as powerful as a recommendation from a friend, customer reviews go a long way in giving a brand credibility and persuading prospective customers that you're a credible and trustworthy company. Many companies automate the collection of reviews with something as simple as sending an email to customers requesting a review a short time after the customer has received the product.

3. **New revenue.** With a community of existing customers, you have a new, more affordable marketing channel for bringing in additional revenue. They've purchased from you once. If they are satisfied and the new offer you present makes sense, they're likely to purchase from you again. Start to plan your strategies for how to provide more value to these customers and, as a result, generate more revenue for your business.

Keep digging for gold

We live in a world that's constantly changing, innovating, and growing. While there were limits on the available gold for those who went to California seeking fortune in 1849, that's not the case for entrepreneurs. As long as you can innovate and evolve the value you provide to society over time, the pool of people who need your offer(s) is unlikely to ever run dry, even for those launching the most niche of products.

Therefore, your responsibility lies in not just catering to the gold you've already found but also in finding more precious metal. It could be new countries you can ship to, new product lines to develop, or new marketing channels to experiment with. What's more, you can create your own gold. Evolutions of, or accessories to, existing products you've successfully sold will allow you to revisit fields of gold you've already mined and find those same fields full, once again, of nuggets.

One real-world example of this strategy that jumps out to me is Bumble, the dating app. Bumble first launched in 2014, only available on iOS and in the United States. It found gold, with many single women attracted to the core app feature that allowed them to send the first message, and Bumble quickly became a key competitor to the big players in the market, such as Tinder and Match.com. The following year, Bumble expanded to new countries and launched their Android app. A year later, they released their first paid product, Bumble Boost. Soon, a new feature, Bumble BFF was released, allowing users to seek friendships rather than romantic relationships, and, not long after, Bumble Bizz was introduced—an app mode for professional networking. Each of these steps is an iteration of their original product, with the goal to further accelerate their growth and find new fields of gold.

Casper, the online mattress startup, is another that comes to mind. When they first launched in 2014, they sold mattresses online. They hit gold, surpassing their year-one revenue goal within two months.[1] In the years that followed, they launched pillows, bed frames, and bedding, and opened up physical stores to support their online efforts. Like Bumble, each of these is a relatively simple iteration of their original gold.

Rinse and repeat

As new ideas take form and your business grows, keep running around that running track. The Five-Step High-Profit Launch System is a learning and feedback loop for establishing how effective a new idea can be.

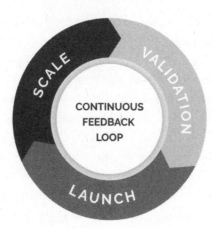

The phases you move through are always the same, regardless of where you are on your business journey:

1. **Validate.** Develop a hypothesis for something you believe to be true, and test it in a simple form. If the data you collect does not match your hypothesis, pivot.
2. **Launch.** When data collected does match your hypothesis, you can roll the hypothesis out more comprehensively.
3. **Scale.** As your hypothesis becomes real, find you gold and watch organic traction begin.

Growth Generators

While you'll likely have leaned heavily on the paid acquisition growth generators for your launch (and perhaps a sprinkling of referral), now's the time to kick all three growth generators into gear.

Paid Acquisition

Paid acquisition refers to presenting your message to customers and acquiring customers through paid channels. While in our digital-first world this tends to mean online advertising, it refers to any effort where your financial investment leads to a tangible growth in customers. The most important thing to remember with paid acquisition as part of a sustainable marketing strategy is that each customer needs to generate profit. This is slightly different to the role of paid acquisition at launch, when entrepreneurs may be prepared to acquire their first customers at a loss due to the credibility, social proof, and longer-term revenue this early traction will generate. Once your business is up and running, profit becomes the priority. As long as you're making a profit on each customer, you can reinvest those profits into more advertising to generate more growth.

Paid Acquisition Pros:

- **Predictability.** Just like the prediction models we ran through toward the end of Chapter 3, any paid acquisition efforts collect core data points that can be used to predict the future.
- **Control.** From the investment you choose to put into this growth generator to the way the prospective customers behave in your funnel, paid acquisition is the growth generator that provides you the most control. You're in charge and can make changes, pull the plug, or put your foot on the gas at any time.

Paid Acquisition Cons:

- **Cost.** Of all the growth generators, this is the one that costs the most financially. Creating and scaling paid acquisition marketing campaigns that generate a strong enough return on your investment isn't easy. It's critical to keep a close eye on data and performance, otherwise you'll burn through a marketing budget in the blink of an eye and potentially with little to show for it.

Paid Acquisition Key Metrics:

- **Cost Per Acquisition (CPA).** The cost to acquire a single paying customer for your business. If you spend $500 on a marketing campaign and get five customers from it, your CPA is $100.
- **Customer Lifetime Value (LTV).** The total worth to your business of a customer over the whole period of their relationship. If the average lifetime relationship of a customer with your business is two years and they tend to buy three products at $250 per product from your company during that period, the LTV is $750.
- **Return-on-Ad Spend (ROAS).** The assessment of your marketing effectiveness, dividing customer lifetime value by your cost per acquisition. If the LTV of a customer is $750 and it costs you $100 to acquire them, the ROAS is 7.50.

Organic Acquisition

This refers to customer acquisition that comes organically over time, such as blog posts, social media marketing, and customers that come back to buy more. This is the process of acquiring new customers without paying any direct fees (such as to an advertising platform).

Organic Acquisition Pros:

- **Cost.** Many people consider it to be free. While you can track any marketing back to some sort of original investment (such as employee time or technology costs), organic acquisition requires a minimal direct financial investment to see returns.
- **Excellence.** For customers to come to your business organically, whether it's a new customer or a returning one, the product generally needs to be of a high quality. Viral and paid acquisition can both acquire customers through sheer force, even if the end product isn't that brilliant, but organic acquisition requires innovation, superiority over competitors, and long-term strategic thinking.

Organic Acquisition Cons:

- **Time.** Generally, organic acquisition occurs naturally as you build your brand and isn't an option for most folks who are just launching. Whether it's new customers finding your business through a blogging strategy or a customer returning for multiple purchases, it takes time.

Organic Acquisition Key Metrics:

- **Customer Retention Rate.** The percentage of customers you can retain over a period of time. It's expressed as a percentage of a company's existing customers who remain loyal within that time frame. For example, if your business has 1,000 customers and, over the course of a two-year period, 200 of those customers come back and buy more, your Customer Retention Rate is 20 percent.
- **Customer Churn Rate.** The percentage of customers you lose over a period of time (the opposite of Customer Retention Rate). For the business that has 1,000 customers and only 200 come back to buy more, their Customer Churn Rate is 80 percent.
- **Customer Acquisition Rate.** The percentage of potential customers, such as website visitors, who actually become customers. In terms of volume, the acquisition of new customers must always exceed the Customer Churn Rate in order for a business to grow.

Viral Acquisition

Here we're referring to growth achieved through user referrals, such as someone sharing your product with their friends. As we saw in Chapter 4, many launch strategies include some form of viral acquisition. It becomes even more important for the long-term success of your business, given the role it can play in reducing your overall marketing expenses (the more you can rely on your customers to spread the word about your business for you, the less you need to rely on your own investment).

Viral Acquisition Pros:

- **Speed.** From the Ice-Bucket Challenge to Gangnam Style to Grumpy Cat, we've all seen the velocity at which popular things can reach millions of people. If your brand successfully implements a viral acquisition program, you'll acquire traction faster than you thought possible and achieve an exponential growth that sets your business up for long-term success.

Viral Acquisition Cons:

- **Difficulty.** It can be incredibly difficult for many products to achieve tangible success with this approach, given you have limited control and impact on whether someone shares your product with their friends via social media or over a lunch conversation. There are ways you can incentivize customers to share (such as providing a future discount or other reward), but, ultimately, you're relying on them to take the necessary action. In general, this type of approach works better with consumer-facing software (such as social media networks like Facebook) versus hardware (such as a physical product you can touch and feel).
- **Control.** When something truly goes viral, it will get out of your control. If the message being promoted about your brand is one you dislike, there's nothing you can do about it. As my mum says: "Be careful what you wish for."

Viral Acquisition Key Metrics:

- **Viral Coefficient.** The number of new customers who are referred by one existing satisfied customer. You get your Viral

Coefficient by multiplying the average number of referrals per customer by the average conversion rate of these referrals. For example, if every customer refers 20 people to your business and 10 percent of those referrals convert into customers, you have a Viral Coefficient of 2.

Grandy's Glorious Bakery Looks to the Future

Let us draw the story of Grandy's Glorious Bakery to a close. Post-launch, Grandy felt excited about the potential of the new venture. What had been an idea at the dinner table just a couple of months earlier was now a real business with real customers and a very real future. With the launch rush period coming to an end, the time arrived for Grandy to be like Franklin. We made a plan to focus on compound interest in a couple of ways:

1. We set up a monthly subscription offer. We offered launch customers the chance to pay a small subscription amount ($10 monthly) to get a box of Grandy's bakes delivered to their door once per month. We called this a Grandy Box. A few dollars a month per customer wasn't a big amount. Over 12 months, though, 50 of these subscriptions would mean an extra $6,000 in revenue.

2. We reintroduced bakes beyond the bestselling coffee cake and coconut jam pastries and launched Grandy Bundles. These were bundles of two or three different but complementary bakes in one order. By offering bundles, we could increase the average transaction value per customer. A 10 percent increase in one order wasn't a big deal, but over 200 orders of $50, an extra 10 percent added $1,000 in revenue.

3. We set up a loyalty (referral) program. Buy a dozen cakes, get one free. Loyalty and referral ("refer a friend") programs can take time to pay dividends. After all, the more customers

you have, the more successful the programs. Building these foundations now will set Grandy in good stead for the future.

Six months later, Grandy and I sat down, enjoyed a slice of coffee cake and a coffee, and talked about a few of the key lessons she'd learned over the course of this journey:

- She didn't need a big financial investment, large swathes of time, or even a finished product in order to validate the idea. What had been a dinner table discussion was, just a few hours later, a business idea being validated in the real world with our Facebook ad funnel and one poster at Grandpa's local golf club.
- What we learned early on about who our customers were and what they wanted had been instrumental in planning the entire business launch (indeed, planning to launch at all!). For instance, if we hadn't set up the "start your order" piece in the validation step, we wouldn't have known: (a) that interest would turn into orders, (b) the types of bakes that would likely be popular, and (c) the amount of money a customer might spend. Setting the right foundations had been vital.
- Resolving customers' questions and issues before they could occur had been critical. This made launch day much, much easier.
- We made the entire process as easy as possible for the potential customers. Simplicity was key.
- Personal touches made all the difference. Yes, the bakes were fantastic. But people also loved Grandy. Her openness, friendliness, cheeky humor, and generous warmth drew people in. Showing the person behind the product had been vital for our successful launch.

After all of this, Grandy said she had a different view of herself. "I believe in myself more now that I'm an entrepreneur," she told me. "Entrepreneurship doesn't have to mean big risk, big investments, and big-headedness. If someone like me can do this, anyone can!"

As Grandy and I finished our slices of cake, her phone rang. A huge order had just come in from a local sports group for their end-of-year awards ceremony.

"Back to work!" Grandy quipped, a marvelous smile spreading across her face. We put the cake away, poured ourselves more coffee, and turned the radio up as she started to prepare her ingredients.

CONCLUSION

Whether you're a new entrepreneur, an experienced business owner, or the journey of entrepreneurship is something you see for yourself in your future, I hope you'll benefit from the insights, strategies, and examples I've shared in this book. Here is a blueprint to take with you:

Entrepreneurship is not exclusive to the biggest risk-takers, the genius college dropouts, or the financially wealthy. It doesn't need a ground-breaking idea, years of back-breaking work, or an investment that'll break the bank. Entrepreneurship is for anyone with an idea that solves a problem, a passion to make that idea a reality, and a willingness to listen and learn.

"Success" in entrepreneurship doesn't mean a Silicon Valley headquarters, a billion dollars in the bank, or a front cover on *Time* magazine. Success is getting up when you fall down and using bumps in the road as launchpads for growth. As a hero of mine, Arnold Schwarzenegger, once said: "Your struggles develop your strengths. When you go through hardships and decide not to surrender, that is strength."

Launch marketing is a methodology that helps entrepreneurs swiftly and affordably prove an idea has the merit and potential to become a profitable business, generate early success for that business, and create a solid foundation for the business to grow.

A key difference between launch marketing and general marketing is the precision and predictability required. While other types of marketing tend to prioritize lots of small improvements over a long period, launch marketing doesn't have the privilege of time or the bandwidth to recover from mistakes.

This is where the Five-Step High-Profit Launch System comes in. It is a recipe for the fast and affordable implementation of launch methodologies, to maximize your chances of success when launching a new product, service, or idea. The system consists of five core steps:

1. Validation, Research, and Strategy
2. Audience Acquisition
3. Audience Engagement
4. Audience Conversion
5. Scale and Optimize

These steps can be bucketed into three key phases. Phase one (consisting of Validation, Research, and Strategy) is about proving there is a market for your idea. Once you've proven there's a market for your idea, you'll enter the second phase (consisting of Audience Acquisition and Audience Engagement), which is about presenting your idea to potential customers before the big launch. Finally, the third phase is when you launch your idea to the world (consisting of Audience Conversion and Scale and Optimize).

Validation, Research, and Strategy recognizes that most new business ideas will fail and guides an entrepreneur through a process to prove their idea has potential for success. You'll define and validate your target audience, your unique value proposition to customers, your messaging, your brand tone, and get a clearer understanding of your go-to market strategy. You'll come out the other side with valuable data that confirms whether the idea can become a profit-generating business well before actually investing much time or money.

Audience Acquisition and Audience Engagement understand that a launch marketing strategy is like an iceberg. The public, visible success at launch is the tip of the iceberg, but it's the work that happens before that success that leads to it—all of the pre-launch work that remains unseen below the surface, finding, acquiring, and engaging your prospective customers. It's vital to truly understand *who* your future customers will be, *what* it is about your solution that makes it better for them than any other solution available, and *why* they will (or will not) make the decision to buy.

As a launch journey proceeds into the third and final phase, entrepreneurs will be faced with new challenges. What sort of launch trajectory will they pursue: the tortoise or the hare? Why might someone express interest in an idea but then opt out? How can launch hurdles be predicted and prevented or solved once they arise? And, most importantly, where do I go from here? After all, a launch is only the beginning.

Being transparent and open will go a long way with your earliest customers. Honesty is always the best policy. It provides solid foundations on which your brand can grow. In the launch marketing world, it may lead to short-term challenges, but it will make up for that in long-term success.

When things go wrong (and they will—no entrepreneur is protected from failure), remember the bigger picture. I recall once when I was struggling with a mistake early in my career, a mentor asked me: "Is this so important that you'll still be thinking about it in two years? If not, don't dwell on it now." This has stayed with me. When failures happen now, I always think of this conversation. The truth is, while it's always painful to fail, 99 percent of your "failures" will be insignificant to you in a couple of years.

Yet while things may go wrong, every entrepreneur will also strike gold. Using HIIT strategies, like Sebastian Coe, and understanding compound growth, like Benjamin Franklin, will enable you to scale your success and create a sustainable, profitable business.

This book has introduced you to my journey, my strategies, the lessons learned, and the stories collected in my years in launch marketing and entrepreneurship. It also shared examples of how other brands have implemented such strategies, focusing not just on the theory of these concepts but the practical side of implementing them, too. Hopefully, you're now equipped with the tools and confidence to pursue your next idea or big entrepreneurial dreams.

I have no doubt you'll succeed. And, as you do, consider how many other aspiring entrepreneurs there are, dreaming of embarking on that adventure but too anxious to do so due to the risk of failure—just like you and I once were. Teach them that entrepreneurship doesn't have to be risky or overwhelming. Allow them to learn from your journey and share that they, too, can do what you've done.

ENDNOTES

Chapter One

1. *Forbes*: "90% of Startups Fail: Here's What You Need to Know About the 10%," 2015 https://www.forbes.com/sites/neilpatel/2015/01/16/90-of-startups-will-fail-heres-what-you-need-to-know-about-the-10/

Chapter Two

1. *Harvard Business Review*: "The Great Repeatable Business Model," 2011: https://hbr.org/2011/11/the-great-repeatable-business-model
2. Ford: Moving Assembly Line: https://corporate.ford.com/articles/history/moving-assembly-line.html
3. Internet World Stats: https://www.internetworldstats.com/emarketing.htm
4. *Statistica*: https://www.statista.com/statistics/266249/advertising-revenue-of-google/
5. Yahoo: "Shopify Announced Third-Quarter 2020 Financial Results," 2020: https://finance.yahoo.com/news/shopify-announces-third-quarter-2020-110000787.html
6. Digital Commerce: US Ecommerce Grows 32.4% in 2020, 2021: https://www.digitalcommerce360.com/article/us-ecommerce-sales

Chapter Three

1. Gustafson, *What Percentage of Businesses Fail.*
2. Statista Research Department: Successfully Funded Kickstarter Projects, 2021: https://www.statista.com/statistics/288345/number-of-total-and-repeat-kickstarter-project-backers/
3. *The Wall Street Journal*: Sue Shellenbarger, "Use Mirroring to Connect with Others," September 20, 2016: https://www.wsj.com/articles/use-mirroring-to-connect-with-others-1474394329
4. *Journal of Consumer Research* 34, no. 6: Robin J. Tanner, Rosellina Ferraro, Tanya L. Chartrand, James R. Bettman, and Rick Van Baaren, "Of

Chameleons and Consumption: The Impact of Mimicry on Choice and Preferences," 2008: https://doi.org/10.1086/522322

Chapter Five

1. "How to Reduce Shopping Cart Abandonment by Optimizing Checkout Process," *Beeketing*, 2018, accessed April 18, 2021: https://beeketing.com/blog/optimize-checkout-process-to-reduce-shopping-cart-abandonment/
2. Primary reason for digital shoppers in the United States to abandon their carts as of November 2018, *Statistica*, 2021: https://www.statista.com/statistics/379508/primary-reason-for-digital-shoppers-to-abandon-carts/
3. "Trust or Bust: Why Trust Seals Can Make or Break a Sale," *Instapage*, 2021: https://instapage.com/blog/website-trust-seals
4. *Inc Magazine*, 2016: https://www.inc.com/kenny-kline/new-study-reveals-just-how-important-brand-transparency-really-is.html
5. Consumer Trust in Online, Social and Mobile Advertising Grows, Nielsen: https://www.nielsen.com/us/en/insights/article/2012/consumer-trust-in-online-social-and-mobile-advertising-grows/
6. Harvard Business School, 2012: https://www.hbs.edu/faculty/Pages/item.aspx?num=40853

Chapter Six

1. Kevin McSpadden, "You Now Have a Shorter Attention Span Than a Goldfish," *Time*, May 14, 2015, https://time.com/3858309/attention-spans-goldfish/
2. "27 Eye-Opening Website Statistics: Is Your Website Costing You Clients?" *Sweor*, February 8, 2021, https://www.sweor.com/firstimpressions
3. "What Do Consumers Really Think About Personalization," *Business2Community*, 2019: https://www.business2community.com/consumer-marketing/what-do-consumers-really-think-about-personalization-02212870

Chapter Seven

1. Customer Acquisition vs. Retention Costs, *Invespcro*, 2021: https://www.invespcro.com/blog/customer-acquisition-retention/
2. *Outbound Engine*, "Customer Retention Marketing vs. Customer Acquisition Marketing": https://www.outboundengine.com/blog/customer-retention-marketing-vs-customer-acquisition-marketing/

Chapter Eight

1. "How Casper's Founders Went from $100,000 in debt to Building a Billion-Dollar Mattress Start-Up," CNBC: https://www.cnbc.com/2019/04/05/how-caspers-founders-built-a-billion-dollar-mattress-start-up.html

INDEX

ABOUT THE AUTHOR

In 2016, Will Russell entered the e-commerce launch space working as a crowdfunding marketing consultant. Multiple six and seven-figure launches that first year meant that client interest—and the need for a larger team—quickly grew.

In 2017, he launched Russell Marketing: an innovative digital agency, specializing in e-commerce launch marketing. To-date, they have generated more than $20 million in revenue for 300+ new entrepreneurs. Will has been featured on Forbes, Business Insider, Crain's New York, StartUp Nation, and more.

In 2021, Will launched the Russell Gives Foundation, a family foundation that offers grants and mentorship to 501(c)(3) partners committed to diversity, equity, and inclusion.

Prior to product launches, Will spent his early career managing launch marketing efforts for brands and websites in the media and non-profit space. A decade of experience in launch marketing—across an array of industries, products, and for businesses of all sizes—provided Will with a unique perspective on the attributes of successful launch campaigns.